PEACE IS ᾽ ᾽ Ὰ Y

A Guide to Pacifist Views and Actions

Compiled and Edited by

Cyril Wright and Tony Augarde

for the Peace Pledge Union

The Lutterworth Press
Cambridge

The Lutterworth Press
P.O. Box 60
Cambridge, CB1 2NT

British Library Cataloguing in Publication Data
Peace is the Way: A guide to Pacifist Views and Actions.
1. Pacifism
I. Wright, Cyril II. Augarde, Tony III. Peace Pledge Union
372.172
ISBN 0-7188-2821-6

First published by The Lutterworth Press, 1990

Printed and bound in Great Britain by
The Guernsey Press Co. Ltd., Guernsey, Channel Islands.

CONTENTS

PREFACE

Pacifism is a temper of the mind which, in a world militarised up to potential total self-destruction, is itself politically powerless and inescapably at odds with society. Yet, despite its powerlessness and the tiny numbers of people it entails, this unbreakable commitment deeply disturbs the military mind. The social sanctions against pacifism seem disproportionately violent, varying only according to the degrees of tolerance or intolerance of the government or other organisation enforcing them.

Extreme militarisation is a product of divisions across the globe into self-righteous groups and it might seem that catastrophe was the sole, inevitable outcome. But the very technology that produces the weapons operates for other purposes - for example, in information technology. Thus we have had TV pictures of American students planting flowers in the barrels of guns; of people in the streets of Prague arguing unarmed with tanks; and now, as I write, of a single student in Beijing, standing alone against a column of tanks, with no power but his individual mind and agility. These pictures have become unexpected and tremendous icons of the pacifist temperament, frail yet strong.

In every generation there has always been a group of people dedicated to the work of clarification, education, moral persuasion. The promotion of peace is their simple objective. Some, such as Gandhi or Luther King, have come right to the forefront of our civilisation. All of them are helping to turn a mass of people across the world away from the military path. This is what this book is about. It has to be written for each generation anew, and for now, with the knowledge of day.

Michael Tippett
1989

Acknowledgements

We are very grateful to all the people who have contributed articles without receiving a fee, and to those who encouraged us in putting this book together: notably Adrian Brink, Linda Yeatman and David Game of Lutterworth Press, and the PPU's National Council and Campaign and Development Committee - especially Rachel Hope, Albert Beale, William Hetherington and Jan Melichar. We are particularly grateful to Sir Michael Tippett for writing the preface.

Acknowledgements also to the Fellowship of Reconciliation and *Peace News* for permission to use previously published material; and to Joan Baez (*'What Would You Do?'*, © 1966, 1968), Sir Michael Tippett (*Contracting-in to Abundance,* 1944), Adam Curle, Ruth Leger Sivard (*World Military and Social Expenditures*, 1988) and Dr Ronald Sampson for permission to use extracts from their writings.

Introduction

Pacifism signifies different things to different people. It can mean simply opposition to war, or conscientious objection to joining the armed forces. It can also be widened to include opposition to all kinds of violence, and hence to oppression and exploitation - which are often called 'structural violence'. Pacifism can involve not only refusing to fight but also nonviolently resisting what is regarded as evil. And pacifism has a very positive side: the belief that only by creating, here and now, peaceful relationships, can we find ourselves on the way to peace. At its widest, it is a whole way of life.

If the views in this book range widely and even differ on some points, this reflects the fact that pacifism is a working hypothesis rather than a fixed creed. Indeed, it is natural for pacifism not to be a rigid ideology, for ideologies often cause conflict and lead to wars. The diverse opinions in this book suggest that pacifism - although it may begin by saying ''No'' to war - is essentially open-minded and open-ended.

Peace is the Way aims to provide an exploration of pacifism through some people's views of what it is, and what it implies for our lives. It includes contributions by all kinds of pacifists and some who might not adopt the name. This book has been compiled by members of the Peace Pledge Union, but it does not necessarily represent the views of the PPU.

The book is divided into several sections so that people, if they wish, may be selective in their reading. It starts with the basis of pacifism and proceeds to answer some questions that are frequently asked in criticism of pacifist attitudes. It then moves to the basic task of addressing the implications that pacifist ideas have for various areas of society. This is the core of the book.

It is followed by a description of some typical examples of actions which pacifists have taken, and then looks at some of the possible alternatives that have been proposed or tried as experiments in creating a peaceful society.

The role of peacemaker belongs to all those who work for

peace. The fifth section highlights the efforts and achievements of some people in this field, who have been a continuing source of inspiration. The main pacifist organisations are listed, together with a guide to finding out about the broader peace movement. The final section imagines how the future might look if pacifist ideas were adopted.

Cyril Wright and Tony Augarde

1. WHAT IS PACIFISM?

An introduction to pacifist ideas and ideals

Stop, You're Killing Me

Tony Augarde

A pacifist is a person who is opposed to war and violence. Pacifists believe that we should not kill or harm other people. And if killing is wrong, war must be wrong - because war is basically a matter of killing. Bertrand Russell pointed out that "patriots always talk of dying for their country, but never of killing for their country". Yet that is ultimately what war means: being prepared to kill other people and inflict suffering on them.

Have we the right to inflict suffering on others? If you think the answer might be "yes" (or "yes - in certain circumstances"), ask yourself if you would like to suffer in the way that people do because of other people's violence. For example, would you like to have petrol poured over you and set alight, so that you either die by burning or live in agony for a few days while your skin peels off? If you don't fancy suffering that sort of death, what makes you think you could ever be justified in dropping napalm bombs on people, since that is exactly the effect of napalm?

Or put it another way. Who is the person you love most? Your mother? Your father? Your wife or husband? Your boy-friend or girl-friend? Your child? How would you feel about that person dying a horrible death as a result of someone's violence? Think about it, and then ask yourself if you still feel justified in using violence on other people. Because, whoever that person is, he or she is someone's child and has a mother, father or loved one to grieve over them, or children who will be left as orphans.

All I am trying to do here is to apply the Golden Rule: do to others as you would wish them to do to you. And it always has the implication: don't do to others what you would not like them to do to you. The world's religions disagree about many things but most of them agree that the Golden Rule is a good general guide to the way we should behave towards others.

And what about the religious viewpoint? What has religion to tell us about the rights and wrongs of violence? You may not be a Christian - many pacifists are not - but Christian morals are widely accepted as a guide to behaviour, so what can they tell us?

The Sermon on the Mount sums up Jesus' basic attitude: "Resist not evil: but whosoever shall smite thee on the right cheek, turn to him the other also . . . Love your enemies, bless them that curse you, do good to them that hate you, and pray for them which despitefully use you and persecute you".

Yet many people will argue that war is sometimes necessary to protect our families and fellow-citizens, or to defend such values as freedom, justice and peace. But how can war protect these things when it is itself a denial of freedom, justice and peace?

War may bring a sort of freedom to one group of people, but usually only at the expense of other people's freedom. In war, the side that 'wins' is not the one with the most justification but the one with the greatest power. And the idea that you can get peace by fighting a war is about as sensible as planting weeds and expecting flowers to grow.

Far from ensuring peace, war creates new problems, such as leaving the vanquished to feel resentful so that they will want to get revenge in the future. We know from our everyday lives that, if we want people to live peaceably with us, it is best to be friendly - not threatening - towards them. So why should we think that in international affairs it is possible to keep the peace by threatening or using war?

Pacifists are often asked such questions as "What would you have done about Hitler?" - implying that some people are so evil that we need to use armed force to resist them. But Hitler was evil because he believed in violence and militarism, which led him (and his followers) to have so little respect for the lives and individuality of others. Pacifists believe in resisting evil - but nonviolently - and they would echo Albert Schweitzer's emphasis on the importance of "reverence for life". If we abhor Hitler because he killed people, how can it be right for us to kill people?

We talk about the sanctity of life, especially when we go to war supposedly to protect the sacred lives of our compatriots, but if there is such a thing as the sanctity of life, it surely applies to everybody, whether they are on our side or not. War conceals this basic truth from us by making us think of other people as 'enemies' rather than as fellow human beings.

It does not make sense that someone should become my enemy just because my government tells me so, particularly when in wartime someone who is our 'enemy' one minute is likely to become our 'friend' the next. During the Second World War, the Russians were our enemies until June 1941, when they became our allies until the end of the war. Then they again became our enemies or, at least, a 'threat' against whom we had to build up huge stocks of armaments. Albert Camus said: ''We are asked to love or hate such and such a country and such and such a people. But some of us feel too strongly our common humanity to make such a choice''.

War is an unsuitable way for humans to solve their differences. And preparations for war deprive humans of many things that they need. Britain spends about £20,000 million a year on armaments and the armed forces - more than it spends on health or education. (If £20,000 million a year is too large a sum for you to visualise, try £400 million a week, or £2 million an hour, or £30,000 a minute.) Meanwhile, thousands of people are homeless, hospitals are understaffed and schools have inadequate resources.

While two-thirds of the world's population is undernourished, the governments of the world spend more than a million dollars a minute on armaments. And what do we get in return for this huge expenditure? Certainly not peace - there have been countless wars since 1945. What we have got is a situation where Russia and America between them have enough nuclear weapons to kill all the people on earth four times over. Does that make you feel happy?

The pacifist believes that war and violence are inhumane, impractical, immoral, unjust and wasteful. What has the pacifist got to offer in their place? Nonviolence - the very opposite of violence.

This doesn't just mean not using violence; it also means a search for positive ways of solving conflicts and achieving real peace: a situation where everybody is allowed all human rights and full opportunity for development and growth.

The first step may appear to be a negative one: to refuse to use violence and to restrict yourself to nonviolent methods in everything you do. Perhaps this seems negative but it can be a very positive thing just to refuse violence, particularly in a world where so many people make excuses for using violence so often. The most positive aspect of nonviolence is that it is a truly moral way, and therefore it is right to be nonviolent however many difficulties this may produce for ourselves. If something is right, we should do it, and do it now, regardless of what everyone else does.

In advocating nonviolence, the pacifist is at a disadvantage because violence has often been tried but nonviolence has been tried much less often, and there is therefore less evidence that it 'works'. Pacifists can point to the success of nonviolent campaigns by such people as Gandhi in India, Dolci in Sicily, and Martin Luther King in America. But pacifists don't pretend to know all the answers. They cannot put forward nonviolence as a tried and tested method guaranteeing success, but as an idea worth trying because it is free from the harmful qualities of violence, because it is a more moral and humane method than violence, and because it conceivably could work.

Once people decide to oppose war and violence by becoming pacifists, there are many ways of working for peace. Possibly the first step is to state clearly one's personal refusal to contribute to war and violence. Regardless of what other people may do or say, you have the power to make your own personal declaration of unilateral disarmament. You can do this by joining the Peace Pledge Union and signing its pledge to "renounce war and never support or sanction another", or you may join one of the other pacifist organisations, or become a conscientious objector, or simply tell yourself that you will have nothing more to do with violence.

Many pacifists see such personal statements or actions as only the first step - though an important one. Pacifists may engage in spreading the truth about war and peace or trying to educate people (including themselves) about these matters; they may take part in demonstrations; they may refuse to pay taxes that buy armaments; or they may engage in other forms of civil disobedience.

They will often work to improve society and remove the

causes of war - injustice, exploitation, the repression of minorities. Some work politically, trying to influence governments on national or international issues. Others, who believe that people have to learn how to improve their own immediate situation, work on a smaller scale in their own localities. All these different ways of working stem from the pacifist's wish to move from a society where war and violence are taken for granted, to a situation where peace is not only what people seek but also the only method they use in trying to move forward. Pacifists believe that "There is no way to peace: peace is the way".

The pacifist tries to break out of the vicious circle of selfishness, greed, aggression and revenge. Perhaps one way to start breaking this circle is to examine one's own responsibility for the violence that exists in the world.

Most of us would claim that we believe in the family of humanity, and the sanctity of life, and loving our neighbours as ourselves. Yet the majority of us are ready to go back on these ideals as soon as our government tells us that somebody is our enemy, or as soon as we feel threatened, or as soon as we allow fear and unreason to get the better of us.

The future of the world depends on us all ceasing to be content with just saying we believe in these ideals. We must start to put them into practice.

Pacifism

Hugh Underhill

Vision and compassion are the imaginative well-springs of the pacifist idea. Compassion prescribes the desirability of the abolition of war, vision its possibility.

The compassion of pacifism is suffering, even despair, and a sense of identity with all suffering and despair. It is an exploration of the humanity within us in its strengths and weaknesses, and a reaching out to the humanity in others, affirming the precept, "As ye would that men should do to you, do ye also to them likewise". This imaginative projection of self into the condition of another human individual or group, concurs with a passionate concern to alleviate suffering and to oppose its causes.

The vision is a glimpse of how it could be - a divination of a peaceful world and how it might come about. It is a willingness to look beyond the expediencies and exigencies of the immediate to more permanent realities, more far-reaching potentials, of the human disposition.

The following passage by Louis Nazzi, a French writer who died young just before the First World War, is remarkably expressive of pacifist vision and compassion:

I hate war, violently, with all my filial and fierce love of life. From the day when I understood the work of faith, ardour, and suffering that is summed up in the single word, life, I have refused my consent to war, which at school I was taught to venerate. When one thinks of the amount of goodwill, tenderness, devotion, fruitless effort, anxious and vigilant thought, toilsome deeds, and tiresome marches, requisite to the filling of a man's existence from the cradle to the grave, one cannot admit its criminal destruction in the name of an interest declared superior. No reason can triumph over it. Nothing can make me deny the individual; I am for him, against sanguinary czars and republics.

Persistent attempts have been made to discredit pacifism as naive and unrealistic. But to pacifists it is the war method and the way of violence which appear to be rooted in the crude emotions of fear and vengeance, in prejudice and unreason, and to stem from an unrealistic assessment of human psychology and needs, and of long-term interests. Pacifism is based on reason and reality, building the firm structure which underpins and ultimately fuses with the pacifist vision and compassion.

Alex Comfort has seen pacifism as having the clearest relevance to historical realities. One may note here the insistence on pacifism as a counter-force to totalitarianism:

> Pacifism is a historical attitude, and it can only be judged historically. Either it is true by the standard of history or it is not - there is no mystique about it: if it is to live, it will be because it is historically and sociologically in accordance with fact, not because it is beautiful or on the side of God or the angels. Either it is a practical policy to attack tyranny by means of individual disobedience and resistance or not. The tenets which, to my mind, make up the political expression of pacifism are these: that every appeal to organised force, by its inevitable degeneration into irresponsibility, is a counter-revolutionary process, and tends to produce tyranny: that the only effective answer to total regimentation is total disobedience; and that there is nothing which is more disastrous than contemporary war - nothing which can make war a 'lesser evil'.

Martin Luther King has also given reasons for thinking that the nonviolent way is the practical and realistic one:

> Violence is impractical, because the old eye-for-an-eye philosophy ends up leaving everybody blind . . . It is immoral because it is a descending spiral ending in destruction for everybody.
>
> Means and ends are inseparable. The means represent the ideal-in-the-making; in the long run of history, destructive means cannot bring about constructive ends.

These appeals to reason agree in suggesting two things: that pacifism will be vindicated by long-term historical realities; and that realism and morality are finally coincident - that what is wrong is also impractical. Our real interests are best served by non-violence.

Moreover, the whole pacifist idea grows out of the recognition of a certain set of realities about human psychology, and about our political and social behaviour, which non-pacifists seem to find difficult to grasp. This can be briefly represented as follows:

Violence breeds violence. Strike somebody and their immediate reaction is to strike back. If they are not able to, they will wait until the opportunity occurs. Punishment and retribution often magnify conflict. They are seldom related to justice. Human nature has a powerful drive towards self-justification, and crude vengeance is easily given a moral colouring. Further, the natural urge is not simply to return an offence in equal measure but to retaliate as devastatingly as possible.

Fear, suspicion and bitterness - like envy and greed - feed upon and regenerate themselves. The deterrence concept sustains an atmosphere unlikely to produce harmonious relationships. Negotiation from strength is a contradiction in terms: threats and counter-threats are not negotiation. Similarly, repressive and authoritarian concepts of civil order tend only to inflame and entrench antagonisms. The use of force does not solve problems: human problems whether individual or international are invariably too complex to be settled by brute force. It merely imposes arbitrary settlements which sooner or later must break down again.

But if pacifism is based on reason and reality, it has to respond positively to two sets of questions which seem to most people overwhelmingly real and reasonable.

To many ordinary people, pacifism appears unsatisfactory because it does not provide readily understandable, immediately useable, or clearly effective methods of dealing with the realities of the world as they have experienced them in their own lives.

Secondly, given that the way of peace and nonviolence is best, how do we actually set about abolishing war and violence?

It would be disingenuous for pacifists to pretend that we know all the answers, or indeed that we have any full or infallible response to the questions. The way in which we can meet the questions is with this insight or understanding: if human suffering and exploitation are to be in any degree reversed, and if our potentiality as a uniquely creative phenomenon is to be redeemed, a way must be found of superseding war and violence. In the full awareness and sensitivity to our common humanity, it is impossible to deliberately kill or inflict suffering for any reason. The effort must be made to carry out the implications of nonviolence in one's personal life, to develop a nonviolent discipline of living. In any case, even those who justify war preparations have to come to terms with such immediate and concrete facts as the extent to which such preparations deprive millions of people of any improvement in living standards, or the unspecifiable dangers involved in manufacturing, testing and storing modern weapons - nuclear, chemical, biological.

Prompted by this insight, pacifists have embarked on extensive studies of the psychological, social, economic and political causes of war, and have enquired into practical steps towards removing these causes, as well as methods of bringing about resolution of actual conflicts. But pacifists have learned above all that the conditions which perpetuate those causes must somehow be changed: we need new patterns and habits of life.

Pacifists vary considerably in the degree and character of change that they conceive to be necessary. Some call themselves 'nonviolent revolutionaries'; some incline towards anarchist solutions; some are in the main stream of liberal humanism; some are relatively conservative in their attitudes. But throughout this spectrum it is recognised that pacifism is at once cause and effect of some kind of mutation in human behaviour, both in the collective and individual spheres.

It is recognised at the same time that power politics and the structures of force, coercion and violence that support them, are simply not going to end quickly, whatever proposals for rational policies may be made. Too many other things have to happen first, and hence pacifists apply themselves nowadays to a very broad field of concern.

The question of exactly how individuals, groups and nations can compass these changes presents pacifists with their essential task. Somehow men and women must be brought into more constructive dialogue with each other, and the often tragic hiatus between the world as it is and the world as we would desire it - though in a sense ineradicable - must be made subject to a more intensive dialectic of change. If the primary psychology of pacifism is a withdrawal from the world as it is into a fantasy of the world as it might be, pacifism is nevertheless a dynamic fact which has affected, and must more positively act upon, reality.

Whether or not we choose to exercise our capability to end war, to redeem civilisation, depends upon the strength of the pacifist will. The pacifist's task is to build this; not to provide all of the answers all of the time, but to generate the will to find the answers, and to create the climate in which they can be found and implemented. This is what organised pacifism is about.

What Would You Do If . . .

Joan Baez

"OK. You're a pacifist. What would you do if someone were, say, attacking your grandmother?"

"Attacking my poor old grandmother?"

"Yeah. You're in a room with your grandmother and there's this guy about to attack her and you're standing there. What would you do?"

"I'd yell 'Three cheers for Grandma!' and leave the room".

"No, seriously. Say he had a gun and he was about to shoot her. Would you shoot him first?"

"Do I have a gun?"

"Yes".

"No, I'm a pacifist, I don't have a gun".

"Well, say you do".

"All right. Am I a good shot?"

"Yes".

"I'd shoot the gun out of his hand".

"No, then you're not a good shot".

"I'd be afraid to shoot. Might kill Grandma".

"Come on. OK, look. We'll take another example. Say you're driving a truck. You're on a narrow road with a sheer cliff on your side. There's a little girl standing in the middle of the road. You're going too fast to stop. What would you do?"

"I don't know. What would *you* do?"

"I'm asking you. You're the pacifist".

"Yes, I know. All right, am I in control of the truck?"

"Yes".

"How about if I honk my horn so she can get out of the way?"

"She's too young to walk. And the horn doesn't work".

"I swerve around to the left of her, since she's not going anywhere".

"No, there's been a landslide".

"Oh. Well then. I would try to drive the truck over the cliff and save the little girl".

Silence.

"Well, say there's someone else in the truck with you. Then what?"

"What's my decision have to do with my being a pacifist?"

"There's two of you in the truck and only one little girl".

"Someone once said, 'If you have a choice between a real evil and a hypothetical evil, always take the hypothetical one'."

"Huh?"

"I said why are you so anxious to kill off all the pacifists?"

"I'm not. I just want to know what you'd do if . . ."

"If I was with a friend in a truck driving very fast on a one-lane road approaching a dangerous impasse where a ten-month-girl is sitting in the middle of the road with a landslide one side of her and a sheer drop-off on the other".

"That's right".

"I would probably slam on the brakes, thus sending my friend through the front windshield, skid into the landslide, run over the little girl, sail off the cliff and plunge to my own death. No doubt Grandma's house would be at the bottom of the ravine and the truck would crash through her roof and blow up in her living room where she was finally being attacked for the first, and last, time".

"You haven't answered my question. You're just trying to get out of it . . ."

"I'm really trying to say a couple of things. One is that no one knows what they'll do in a moment of crisis. And that hypothetical questions get hypothetical answers. I'm also hinting that you have made it impossible for me to come out of the situation without having killed one or more people. Then you can say 'Pacifism is a nice idea, but it won't work'. But that's not what bothers me".

"What bothers you?"

"Well, you may not like it because it's not hypothetical. It's real. And it makes the assault on Grandma look like a garden party".

"What's that?"

"I'm thinking about how we put people through a training process so they'll find out the really good, efficient ways of killing. Nothing incidental like trucks and landslides . . . Just the killing. Nothing incidental like trucks and landslides . . . Just the opposite, really. You know, how to growl and yell, kill and crawl and jump out of airplanes . . . Real organised stuff. Hell, you have to be able to run a bayonet through Grandma's middle''.

''That's something entirely different''.

''Sure. And don't you see that it's so much harder to look at, because it's real, and it's going on right now? Look. A general sticks a pin into a map. A week later a bunch of young boys are sweating it out in a jungle somewhere, shooting each other's arms and legs off, crying and praying and losing control of their bowels . . . Doesn't it seem stupid to you?''

''Well, you're talking about war''.

''Yes, I know. Doesn't it seem stupid?''

''What do you do instead, then? Turn the other cheek, I suppose''.

''No. Love thine enemy but confront this evil. Love thine enemy. Thou shalt not kill''.

''Yeah, and look what happened to him''.

''He grew up''.

''They hung him on a damn cross is what happened to him. I don't want to get hung on a damn cross''.

''You won't''.

''Huh?''

''I said you don't get to choose how you're going to die. Or when. You can only decide how you're going to live. Now''.

''Well, I'm not going to go letting everybody step all over me, that's for sure''.

''Jesus said, 'Resist not evil'. The pacifist says just the opposite. He says to resist evil with all your heart and with all your mind and body until it has been overcome''.

''I don't get it''.

''Organised nonviolent resistance. Gandhi. He organised the Indians for nonviolent resistance and waged nonviolent war against the British until he'd freed India from the British Empire. Not bad for a first try, don't you think?''

''Yeah, fine, but he was dealing with the British, a civilised people. We're not''.

''Not a civilised people?''

''Not dealing with a civilised people. You just try some of that stuff on the Russians''.

''You mean the Chinese, don't you?''

"Yeah, the Chinese. Try it on the Chinese".

"Oh dear. War was going on long before anybody dreamed up Communism. It's just the latest justification for self-righteousness. The problem isn't Communism. The problem is consensus. There's a consensus out that it's OK to kill when your government decides who to kill. If you kill inside the country, you get in trouble. If you kill outside the country, right time, right season, latest enemy, you get a medal. There are about 130 nation-states, and each of them thinks it's a swell idea to bump off all the rest because he is more important. The pacifist thinks there is only one tribe. Five billion members. They come first. We think killing any member of the family is a dumb idea. We think there are more decent and intelligent ways of settling differences. And we had better start investigating those other possibilities because, if we don't, then by mistake or by design, we will probably kill off the whole damn race".

"It's human nature to kill".

"Is it?"

"It's natural. Something you can't change".

"If it's natural to kill, why do men have to go into training to learn how? There's violence in human nature, but there's also decency, love, kindness. Man organises, buys, sells, pushes violence. The nonviolenter wants to organise the opposite side. That's all nonviolence is: organised love".

"You're crazy".

"No doubt. Would you care to tell me the rest of the world is sane? Tell me that violence has been a great success for the past five thousand years, that the world is in fine shape, that wars have brought peace, understanding, brotherhood, democracy and freedom to mankind and that killing each other has created an atmosphere of trust and hope. That it's grand for one billion people to live off the other four billion, or that even if it hasn't been smooth going all along, we are now at last beginning to see our way through to a better world for all, as soon as we get a few minor wars out of the way".

"I'm doing OK".

"Consider it a lucky accident".

"I believe I should defend America and all that she stands for. Don't you believe in self-defence?"

"No, that's how the Mafia got started. A little band of people who got together to protect peasants. I'll take Gandhi's non-

23

violent resistance''.

"I still don't get the point of nonviolence''.

"The point of nonviolence is to build a floor, a strong new floor, beneath which we can no longer sink. A platform which stands a few feet above napalm, torture, exploitation, poison gas, A and H bombs, the works. Give man a decent place to stand. He's been wallowing around in human blood and vomit and burnt flesh, screaming how it's going to bring peace to the world. He sticks his head out of the hole for a minute and sees an odd bunch of people gathering material and attempting to build a structure above ground in the fresh air. 'Nice idea but not very practical' he shouts and slides back into the hole. It was the same kind of thing when man found out the world was round. He fought for years to have it remain flat, with every proof on hand that it was not flat at all. It had no edge to drop off or sea monsters to swallow up his little ship in their gaping jaws''.

"How are you going to build this practical structure?''

"From the ground up. By studying, learning about experimenting with every possible alternative to violence on every level. By learning how to say no to the nation-state, no to war taxes, 'NO' to the draft, 'NO' to killing in general, 'YES' to the brotherhood of man, by starting new institutions which are based on the assumption that murder in any form is ruled out, by making and keeping in touch with nonviolent contacts all over the world, by engaging ourselves at every possible chance in dialogue with people, groups, to try to begin to change the consensus that it's OK to kill''.

"It sounds real nice, but I just don't think it can work''.

"You are probably right. We probably don't have enough time. So far we've been a glorious flop. The only thing that's been a worse flop than the organisation of nonviolence has been the organisation of violence''.

2. PACIFISM AND SOCIETY

How pacifists look at various aspects of society: the implications of pacifism for some areas of life

Militarism

William   Hetherington

It is the eternal complaint of military historians that Britain has never enjoyed militarism. It is not suggested by this that Britain has ever pursued a particularly pacifist policy, but rather that the British were traditionally wary of a standing army.

It is true that Britain continued much longer than France or Prussia, for example, the practice of raising armies *ad hoc* as wars occurred and then disbanding them. It is perhaps salutary to reflect that amongst the reasons for the overthrow of James II in 1688 was his ''raising and keeping a standing army within this kingdom in time of peace and quartering soldiers contrary to law''. That, however, has not prevented Parliament from annually renewing the Crown authority for maintaining a standing army ever since that time.

Britain has fortunately never reached the stage of 18th and 19th century Prussia where, it has been said, the state existed round and for the army (compulsory military service for men being introduced in 1733). We saw with the introduction of conscription in 1916 and its reintroduction in 1939, combined with the direction of both male and female civilian labour, the emergence - for periods at least - of a state as completely committed to war as Kaiser Wilhelm's and Hitler's Germanies, the lineal descendants of the selfsame Prussia.

What, then, is militarism? What are the values it connotes? The first is authoritarianism - blind obedience to leaders by the

25

led. It is only by this means that people can be induced to kill strangers with whom they have no personal quarrel and to expose themselves to slaughter: ''theirs not to reason why, theirs but to do and die''. If one looks for a more significant example than the Light Brigade of the Crimea, with one hundred and fifty-seven dead in one futile charge, what about the Somme in 1916 with nineteen thousand dead in just the first of one hundred days?

Authoritarianism itself is dependent upon elitism. Nowhere is the hierarchy of class more rigidly maintained than in the armed services: all human contact between 'officers' and 'men' is avoided to keep the divide between the leaders and the led.

The third component of militarism may be called dehumanising or brutalising of feeling. The soldier (or sailor or airman) is essentially a machine for killing, maiming and destroying; ordinary human emotions must not be allowed to interfere. Whether it is training soldiers to shoot at cut-out human figures, forbidding any repetition of the Christmas 1914 truce in which soldiers of opposing armies sang and exchanged gifts with each other, or ordering the dropping of a bomb to wipe out a whole city in one blinding flash; one must be indoctrinated never to think of the 'enemy' as real people. If in the process this breeds brutality to one's comrades, an occasional scapegoat may be sacrificed to public concern.

Militarism thus represents the totalitarian state in microcosm: absolute authority in a rigid hierarchy with no ultimate respect for human life or feeling. This applies equally to regular and guerilla armies, whether pursuing 'imperialist' or 'liberationist' aims. When the dictionary defines militarism as the exaltation of military force, it is these values and attitudes which are being glorified, honoured, feted and held out as examples to be emulated or experiences to be enjoyed.

The inculcation of militarism begins early in life. From lead soldiers to Action Man (the sexist equivalent of dolls for non-cissy boys), from miniature pistols to life-size plastic bazookas, from war 'comics' to sophisticated 'war games'; children in general, and boys in particular, are subjected to military influence. Cadet forces, virtually compulsory in some schools, provide explicit military training, including the use of arms, at a highly impressionable age, with subsidies from public funds for clothing, equipment and camps that are available to no other youth organisations.

For those who evade the cadet forces, there are all the exhibitions and fairs which are thought not to be complete unless one or more of the armed forces is present to demonstrate the delights of death and destruction to as young an audience as possible.

Killing, of course, is what the armed forces are all about; whether it is a private soldier gouging the guts out of someone with his bayonet, or a senior officer pressing the button to annihilate a million people in the nuclear holocaust of a guided missile. It is in an attempt to make this job seem as respectable as possible, that the army has chosen the title 'professional'. We need to constantly remind not only ourselves but those who are most likely to be seduced by the glossy recruiting brochures, that beyond the glamour of foreign beaches and the thrill of winter sports lie the bonds of servitude and the spectre of death.

There exists a whole mythology of militarism. It defines as 'peacekeeping' a war in Northern Ireland in which the army has killed scores of men and women and dozens of children; rounded up hundreds for internment without trial, and tortured people under the guise of interrogation. It gives the name 'defence' to rocket-launching sites aimed to destroy half of Europe. It values the barbed-wire fences of military bases more highly than the landscape on which they are built. It cloaks its deadly work in official secrecy. It justifies increases in military expenditure by cutting down on health, social services and education.

It is in the hope that most people can be fooled by these myths most of the time that militarism is officially advanced in all walks of public life. How often is some local civic ceremony accomplished without at least a military band to encourage the belief that soldiering is really rather jolly? Even on Remembrance Day, the gun salutes and military parades contradict the token expression of sorrow and say, in effect, ''we are waiting only for the next war once more to kill or be killed''.

There is, alas, more to militarism than civic pride. The same commercial interests behind war toys fill shelves of 'war books' which have more to do with the glorification of war than historical research or truth-reflecting fiction such as *All Quiet on the Western Front*. The same may be said of films and television programmes. Newspapers present wars as heroic occasions and constantly refer in words and pictures to 'our boys' and the 'fighting spirit'.

In the advertising of non-military goods, militarist images still appear: the army officer served coffee by his Indian servant; the cigarettes supposedly boosted by the navy; nor are the children neglected: a mushroom cloud to sell fruit lozenges; a hand-grenade for a bubble bath. Firms use advertising to contribute directly to a militarist cause, as when a building society puts a 'Battle of Britain' display in its window.

The influence of war upon women must not be overlooked. Boys may be more susceptible to war toys, and men may suffer more through economic or other conscription, but the First World War poster 'The Women of Britain Say Go' shows that their approval makes the continuance of war possible. In these days of total war, the particular role played by either sex becomes less relevant. The choice for or against war must be lived out by each of us in our daily lives.

These are merely some examples of the ways in which our society not only justifies but exalts military force. In campaigning against militarism, we challenge those who still argue for the 'just war' philosophy - that war is sometimes the lesser of two evils - to admit the implication that, if war is thus evil, we have no business to be proud of its men and machines.

Defence

William Hetherington

'Defence' is a major issue between the various political parties in Britain. Each argues the best way and the best weapons to use against a potential 'aggressor' against the United Kingdom or our 'allies'. There is much talk of 'deterring' such an 'enemy' and making it not worth while for aggression to occur. The controversy has further sharpened between those supporting nuclear weapons and those who would rely on 'conventional' weapons.

On the other hand, within the wider peace movement both here and abroad, there is debate about three different ways of defending ourselves. *Alternative defence,* usually meaning non-nuclear defence; *nonviolent civilian defence,* usually meaning preparedness to resist the same sort of 'aggression' that is of concern to politicians, by nonviolent means; and *social defence,* usually meaning nonviolent defence of grassroots communities rather than states. These 'defence' policies are proposed sometimes on moral grounds and sometimes on tactical grounds, but there is frequently the same assumption as is made by the politicians - that without 'defence' policies people generally feel insecure and that the peace movement must have a coherent response to the deeply-felt need for security.

To pacifists, however, this argument seems to begin in the wrong place. Pacifists are naturally opposed to the use of any kind of weapons, nuclear or 'conventional', and to the threat of their use. But we are wary also of aligning with those who argue for 'alternative defence'. The problem lies in the attitude implicit in the language of 'defence': the basic assumption that people are bound to have enemies and must defend themselves from such enemies. We have two questions to raise about such assumptions.

The first is to ask whether the concept of the enemy country is as natural as people are expected to believe. At present the

29

British are led to understand that the Soviet Union is still our main potential enemy. Only a generation ago the people of that country were our allies, whilst the role of the people of West Germany has been changed in the other direction. If we look further back, we can see shifts in the way we were expected to view the French, the Americans, the Spanish.

To take a more recent example, Britain had a short but bloody war with Argentina in defence of the Falkland Islands but, until the day of the invasion, Argentina was regarded as sufficiently friendly to receive armaments from Britain. On the other hand, it was the British navy, defending the Islands, who killed the only three Islanders to die in the conflict.

The second question is to ask whether we should accept the partition of the world into nation states, presupposing a need for each to defend itself against other nation states. The state, indeed, is often spoken of as if it were a person with an individual's concerns, feelings and responses towards other individuals. The phrase 'the national interest' often thinly disguises the assumption that such other individuals are actually or potentially hostile.

Pacifism is based on a very different way of looking at our own society as well as international affairs. It begins with the responsibility that each person has towards creating a society in which everyone can live fully and effectively, with a reasonable share of the world's resources. In talking of society, however, pacifists are concerned on the one hand with relationships between people on a day-to-day basis within their own community and on the other with people seeing others as people regardless of frontiers. The concept of statehood, as opposed to community or people, is essentially divisive, enabling governments on either side to dragoon individual people into killing other individuals with whom they have no personal quarrel.

Is the concept of defence therefore totally irrelevant? We have to ask ourselves what are the really important things to us as people, that we feel are worth defending against anyone who might wish to take them away from us. Put like that, many of us might refer to our family and dearest friends, and then list such intangibles as freedom to meet each other, and speak publicly; the right to work and receive a fair share of material resources; having a home where we can enjoy privacy; access to knowledge and means of developing our ability to learn from what we see and hear; the right to be where we feel we belong.

When we start to consider such a list and ask where the real threat to such ideals comes from, we find that the answer is by no means necessarily a foreign enemy. We could draw up another list of the things that threaten 'our way of life'. The list of threats might well include laws restricting free speech, association or travel; imprisonment for those who nonviolently break such laws; the extortion of tax to pay for weapons and wars that nobody wants as an ordinary person; the indoctrination of children with the idea that other people are enemies; the glorification of war by the media; poverty and homelessness for some whilst money is spent on armaments, and others live in plenty; racism and denigration of one group of people by another; the destruction of our environment.

The immediate threat to most of these things in Britain comes not from the Soviet Union or other foreign powers, but from our own government or from other institutions and people in our society. It should also be made clear that there is no party-political point in the references to government. Left-wing governments have threatened essential freedoms as much as right-wing ones.

It makes personal decision-making easy if you are told that people of a certain country are the enemy. All that has to be done is the hating and if necessary the killing, and all problems will supposedly be solved. It is more difficult to see our own government and the influential people in society as the real threat to our way of life. We are encouraged to see governments as our protectors. When we examine military defence systems, we find that they have more to do with protecting leaders of the country than ordinary people who always suffer on both sides of an armed conflict.

It is not difficult to recall examples of the bitterness and waste created by policies of confrontation and violence: millions without meaningful work; people dying of cold and disease; thousands homeless whilst more prisons are being built; the police being given greater powers whilst governments 'elected' by minorities ignore public protest; the pollution of rivers and forests by profit-motivated industry, and the ravaging of open country by missile bases and military manoeuvres; the ultimate threat to us all of a nuclear catastrophe that was demonstrated so tragically at Chernobyl and was so nearly demonstrated at Windscale but deliberately kept secret for thirty years.

The present defence of most countries including our own, is based on armed force; it relies on people's willingness to use all forms of violence in the hope that such a threat will hold an unstable peace with potential enemies.

This involves huge expenditure on military recruitment and training, on research and development of weapons systems and other equipment, and on the human cost of diverted intellectual and economic resources, both in this country and the developing world. Such a defence policy kills, even before weapons are used.

Pacifists totally reject this form of 'defence' on both moral and pragmatic grounds: it is itself part of the threat against which all people need to defend themselves. It is significant that military training requires people to be brutalised into learning to kill, and that people often have to be conscripted to fight in major wars. We believe that killing can never be used for life-affirming purposes, nor can peace be achieved through war.

We believe that means of action are inseparable from the ends of our action. It has been well said, there is no way to peace - peace is the way. Therefore whilst we are in duty bound to resist threats to our peace and the peace of others, we must do so in a way that respects the essential humanity of all. There is a long tradition of nonviolent resistance in this country, from religious and political persecution of the 17th century to the blockades of cruise missiles today. We have learned much from Gandhi and Martin Luther King, and now new levels and ways of resistance have developed: the refusal of local authorities to co-operate in civil defence; the re-emergent women's nonviolent movement; the withholding of taxes to be spent on war preparations; the reclaiming of land by environmental groups.

It is in this tradition that pacifists take their stand and invite others to join them in exploring new ways of working together and communicating with people both within and across frontiers. In time this will help to bring about the social, political and economic changes which will cause defence to become irrelevant, as people more and more trust rather than fear each other.

Disarmament

Tony Augarde

Most people want disarmament. But how can we achieve it? And how much do we want?

People have been advocating and working for disarmament for many years. Even governments have declared, over and over again, that they would like to disarm. Yet only a few agreements have been made, mostly in areas where the nations had little or nothing to lose. As Jerome Frank has said: "Such negotiations in good faith as there are, tend to be about relinquishing weapons that do not really matter, like obsolete bombers".

The Stockholm International Peace Research Institute (SIPRI) lists only about a dozen arms-control agreements which have been made since 1945. Even these have very doubtful value. The nuclear powers have not met the disarmament obligations they undertook in the Non-Proliferation Treaty. The SALT Anti-Ballistic Missile (ABM) Treaty has limited a specific type of anti-ballistic missile but the development of new ABMs continues.

And yet many calls for disarmament are still only partial - asking, for example, that Trident should not replace Polaris or that Europe should become a nuclear-free zone.

Certainly, partial disarmament is attractive, because it seems easier to achieve than complete disarmament. It may be a good strategy to tackle one or two small advances at a time - if this leads to genuine disarmament. But it seldom does. Robert Johansen in *The Disarmament Process* says: "Although small steps towards a disarmed world appear to be politically easier to take than large ones, thirty years of negotiations for partial measures offer little hope that they will achieve a reversal of the increase in arms". Moves that governments make for partial disarmament, like the SALT talks, may actually be a con-trick: to make the people think governments intend to disarm when little disarmament actually takes place. Perhaps disarmament conferences are devices to forestall public concern rather than to reverse the arms race.

If governments want to disarm, they need not go to conferences. They can start disarming today. When Canada decided to do away with its own nuclear weapons, it did so at once, without waiting for other nations to agree to do the same. In fact, unilateral disarmament is the only kind of disarmament that makes sense. If nations cannot trust one another, no disarmament treaty will ensure that those nations abide by any agreements.

Besides, unilateral disarmament is not only practical - it is a moral imperative. If it is right to disarm, we should do it - whatever other nations do.

But perhaps it is unrealistic to ask *governments* to disarm. Do not governments need armaments because they need enemies, to create unity among their own people, and in the last resort to control the people they rule? On the evidence of the last forty years, governments have little will to disarm. Perhaps we should refuse to make their weapons and refuse to join their armies - and thus *make* them disarm.

If moves for partial disarmament have generally proved futile, is there any hope in asking for complete disarmament? It might at least prevent us from underestimating the magnitude of the problem or overestimating the steps than governments have so far taken towards disarmament. Johansen says: "Advocating general and complete disarmament - rather than partial steps - reminds us of the need to consider fundamental institutional change. In addition, such a posture underscores the need to measure the presently armed world against the goal of a disarmed world, rather than against small steps of arms control which, even if achieved, seem to legitimise the weapons that remain".

How much disarmament do we want? Some people think that nuclear weapons are the most important thing to get rid of. Yet many declarations of disarmament aims - for example, in the covenant of the League of Nations and in the United Nations Charter - have gone as far as demanding "general and complete disarmament", including the disbanding of armed forces, dismantling of military establishments, liquidation of all armaments and the discontinuance of military expenditure.

The mention of military expenditure is a reminder that disarmament concerns more than just nuclear weapons. Professor

Michael Pentz has pointed out that "in purely financial terms, the nuclear arms race accounts for a relatively small proportion of the global arms bill. It costs less than 20% of the military budgets of the great powers and less than 10% of the world's military budget of about 400,000 million dollars".

Nuclear weapons are an immense threat to peace. But if we scrapped all nuclear weapons, we would still be spending a vast amount on 'conventional' weapons, every pound of which is a theft from the world's starving people and a contribution to the build-up of international tension and instability. Moreover, if we scrapped all nuclear weapons, we would still possess the sort of 'conventional' weapons that killed as many people in Dresden and Tokyo as the atomic bomb killed in Hiroshima.

If we are concerned about nuclear weapons because they kill or endanger human beings, should we not also be concerned about *any* weapons that do this? Nuclear weapons are specially criticised for being 'indiscriminate'. Does this mean that we approve of killing which is 'discriminate'? Nuclear disarmers sometimes explain that they oppose 'weapons of mass destruction' but how do you decide what is mass destruction and what is small or acceptable destruction? If killing 100,000 is unacceptable, is it all right to kill 10,000?

Nuclear weapons may currently be the weapons most capable of the greatest destruction, but what of the new weapons which we are even now devising? Biological weapons, for instance, which could destroy all life on earth with only a test-tube full of germs?

Ultimately, it is not particular weapons which are horrible but the inhuman willingness to use such weapons. This is not to deny the strong effect of descriptions of the suffering at Hiroshima and Nagasaki, which suggest the terrible effects of nuclear weapons.

Anyone with humane sympathies is bound to feel revulsion when reading such things as: "The ground was a charred mass of debris and bricks, stones and girders, and bodies pounded to nothing". Or this: "One man, surrounded by corpses, described a loud wailing 'as if huge fingers were being dragged across an enormous glass pane, rising and falling, interminable and unbearable', that came from a muddy sunken road where hundreds of wounded were shouting, moaning, and singing in delirium". These two quotations describe not Hiroshima, but the Battle of the Somme, in 1916.

International Relations

Hilda Morris

A distinction has to be drawn between diplomatic and economic international relations. Economic relations may exist where there are no diplomatic relations or only very tenuous ones, even where two states are openly hostile, in words at least. Even when relations between the United States and Soviet Russia have been frosty, America has been happy to sell its surplus wheat to Russia, and for various reasons the USSR has been forced to buy it. Until recently, East and West Germany officially had only semi-diplomatic relations (they maintained permanent missions but no embassies in each other's capitals), but the trade between them ran into many millions.

Although there is a difference between economic and diplomatic relations, the two often are closely intertwined. One has only to think of the North-South divide, the difficulties engendered by the gulf between the developed and the developing countries. Henry Kissinger wrote in 1983: "If the debt crisis winds up spawning radical anti-Western governments, financial issues will be overwhelmed by the political consequences". In other words, economic factors can, and often do, influence international relations as a whole. Moreover, the giving or withholding of financial aid is used to put pressure on regimes which the potential donor countries wish to win over or punish for political reasons.

It is a truism that technological ingenuity has far outstripped human capacity or willingness to abide by and apply moral values to inter-state relations. There certainly are countries which internally recognise and, to a certain extent, are governed by such values, although even there they are under threat in crisis situations, such as war. However, in international relations self-interest and the most primitive tribal instincts seem to instruct the rulers as well as the peoples. It may be argued that co-operation and mutual understanding are to be found within the various alliances set up by certain nations for specific purposes, but such groupings usually serve specific economic or military ends, e.g. the European Economic Community, Comecon, Nato, the Warsaw Pact, etc. Military alliances naturally have a hostile intent, and economic associations normally include an element of fierce competition, though some go beyond their confines to give aid, for example the EC's Lomé Convention.

There are two important factors which bedevil international relations. One of these is ideology. The world has been split between the communist and the capitalist camps. They both comprise many shades and subdivisions, but generally speaking the enmity between them determines the climate of international relations. They accuse each other of wanting to rule the world, and each - in order to prevent such hegemony - piles armaments upon armaments in a never-ending spiral. In conflict areas, such as the Middle East, South-East Asia and parts of Africa, although hostilities are not always directly concerned with the East-West divide, America and Soviet Russia and their allies decisively influence the relations between the countries concerned, in that they openly or covertly aid and encourage one side or another, according to where their interests lie.

The other factor in international relations concerns internal affairs of countries. Even, or perhaps especially, an oppressive regime is anxious to establish and maintain a measure of consensus with its people, and there is no better way of achieving popular cohesion than a threat from outside. Any friction or disagreement between nations is exaggerated and exploited to divert people's attention from internal difficulties or to gain support for measures which otherwise may be resisted. In that connection, it is worth noting that in some instances diplomatic contacts are maintained and negotiations conducted in secret at the same time as the public is allowed to hear only the childish invectives the governments involved fling at each other in their efforts to uphold the myth of an imminent threat. Any unwanted developments are attributed to sinister 'foreign' influences. The impact of this trend on international relations is obvious: an already tense situation is further inflamed and peaceful negotiations made more difficult. It follows that the internal conditions of every country are of crucial importance for international relations. Oppression and economic injustice lay the body politic open to the virus of dissent and rebellion; and consequently to those external forces which desire to encourage and support revolt, and those which desire to uphold the status quo in their own interests.

Some people, pacifists among them, believe that reasonable international relations will be achieved only with the abolition of the nation state and/or the establishment of world government. Others argue for the introduction of anarchism. All these solutions, of course, are highly controversial. However, there would appear to be some shorter-term measures which, if adopted even by some countries initially, could lead to a great improvement of international relations.

Governments, especially those of the superpowers, should refrain from efforts to 'destabilise' unwanted regimes, from directly or indirectly interfering in international or internal conflicts. Above all, they should not supply arms, troops or military training to governments or 'dissidents' engaged in such conflicts. Financial aid should be made conditional on potential recipients' sincere efforts to find peaceful and equitable solutions to their international or internal problems. In short, aid and support of whatever kind should not depend on the donors' political or military interests.

All governments, even those engaged in military conflict, want peace - on their own terms. They know that those terms are irreconcilable. Their protestations are addressed to the gallery. The same is true of governments involved in negotiations about disarmament or arms control.

International relations will improve when the rulers of the world forget weapon technology and ancient tribalism and remember to serve humanity.

The Third World

Vernon Cutting

World communications bring the 'Global Village' into our homes every day. We may see a state occasion, a flood disaster, space travel, agricultural advance or starving refugees. But the picture moves from view as quickly as it appeared. We are only reminded again of the world's needs by the appeals of charities such as Oxfam and Christian Aid. Do people concerned in such charities always recognise the forces that create the conditions they strive to alleviate?

If one task of pacifism is to stir people to action, this is particularly so about a better life for three-quarters of the world's population, whose background is reflected in UNICEF's statement that 40,000 children under five years of age die unnecessarily each day from hunger and disease.

Why is there such a Rich/Poor divide between the North/South countries of our world? Exploration over the past 500 years revealed new lands and mineral resources that became available to those nations whose sailors found them. Human resources, too, were exploited - the slave trade is reputed to have caused the loss of more than 50 million Africans. These new countries thus provided an 18th and 19th century version of 'Aid', producing wealth for the industrialising countries of the West.

Although political independence was achieved in the 20th century, the same 'neo-colonial' economic factors prevent full development in the Third World. Why should there be starvation in one part of the world while subsidies are given for excessive production in another? What are the problems and the scale of costs in overcoming such anomalies?

When we consider the needs of greater food production to meet increases of population, it is encouraging to see that India is now self-sufficient in cereals, though localised shortages may occur. High-yielding 'Green Revolution' varieties have not always achieved their potential on small farms, due to lack of irrigation and essential fertilisers. These are readily available to the more affluent producers, whose outputs have doubled. The Food and Agriculture Organisation's fertiliser scheme for thirty countries, so vital for utilising research findings, could be funded annually by the operating costs of an anti-submarine cruiser.

The effects of wide variations in climate, from Sahelian drought to Bangladeshi floods, should be alleviated by international food security through local stocks of staple grains. Environmental changes such as the 'greenhouse effect' will make such considerations even more urgent, to reinforce real food security that can only come by strengthening food production in vulnerable areas. Foods customarily in use can thereby be increased, but people also wish to extend the range of their diets. For example, wheat flour is more popular but it often has to be imported in place of the higher-yielding local millets and sorghums which can be less acceptable socially.

While it is vital to increase food production, much of farming effort and the most fertile land is used for export crops such as cotton, palm oil and tea. Research is often concentrated on these commodities, while peasant farmers are without local advisers and marketing facilities.

The desired control of population will be encouraged by improved health services, to reduce child mortality and thus avoid the pressure to raise more children as financial security for their parents' old age.

A major influence in such rural progress is the widening of educational opportunities. Many countries have quadrupled their literacy rate to 80% or more, often through UNESCO's Literacy Project. This six-year worldwide campaign gave specialist support to national inputs, at an overall cost equivalent to merely two fighter aircraft.

Better health will come from the greater resistance to illness afforded by improved diets, but water-borne diseases will still cause 60% of the deaths of children under five years old. Where piped water has been installed in cholera areas, this disease has been reduced by 95%. UNICEF's Water Decade aimed to provide every village in the world with clean water. The over-all cost could readily be met by a 1% cut for ten years in the world's annual arms expenditure.

One cause of blindness is a deficiency of vitamin A. This shortage makes 200,000 children blind each year, but protection can be given to 1,000 children at the small cost of a military pistol.

The greatest recent achievement in disease control was the World Health Organisation's elimination of smallpox. The cost of this technical and educational programme across the world was equivalent to that of only two naval frigates. The WHO scheme of child immunisation against six diseases, including diphtheria, measles and polio, could save a million lives a year for five years by using the cost of a single Trident submarine.

In addition to natural hazards, there are economic and political factors which affect poverty and national stability. Many aspects of life, better housing and hospitals, can only develop by importing essential items. Exports must provide the foreign exchange for these necessities. Producers, however, have little control over commodity markets, and a country's income can be very uncertain. For example, in a decade the amount of fertiliser purchased by the price of a ton of coffee has been halved.

Although higher oil prices benefit Third World countries which produce oil, the 'non-oil' countries are adversely affected. Thus, there has been a ten-fold increase in the amount of sugar needed to pay for one ton of oil.

And yet, so much of this hard-earned foreign exchange is absorbed by disproportionate spending on arms and military forces. Too often, these provide an apparently easy solution to change at a time of political and ethnic instability. Civil wars can be more wasteful and permanently damaging, in proportion, than are international conflicts.

Although all the developing countries account for only one fifth of the world expenditure on arms, this takes a vital part of their budgets. It is not without significance that the arms-supplying nations make 75% of their sales to the Third World. Because of the easier loans frequently offered to cover arms purchases, governments can offer a more assured life to their young people in the army than in many civilian jobs.

This arms production is also detrimental to the economies of the industrialised nations. A major component in Japan's economic success is the fact that all its scientific and technical abilities have been devoted to constructive production for consumption and export, rather than being diverted to weapons manufacture. There is further damage to national economies because military spending offers only half the employment per unit of expenditure as arises from a similar amount spent on education or health.

With the excessive costs of high-overkill conditions, the challenge of saying ''No to war'' is more than ever relevant to unite our world, so divided in outlook and riches.

The Arms Trade

Paul Seed

The arms trade includes both major weapons - such as tanks, planes and warships - and the cheaper but equally deadly small arms and explosives. It also includes the 'dual use' equipment such as radar and communication systems which are essential to a modern army but which also have non-military uses.

The three evils arising from the arms trade in the purchasing country are death through war, death through poverty, and death through governmental repression. The selling country, generally wealthier and more powerful, suffers in less direct ways: through damage to the economy and increased militarism in its own society.

It is sometimes argued that the arms trade and the development of military industries in the Third World help to correct an imbalance between North and South; and that the weapons are in any case very popular with the recipient governments themselves, who see restrictions on the arms trade as an attack on their right to self-defence. If this is so, why are there such massive attempts to promote military sales, and why is the trade opposed by the peoples of recipient countries?

Since 1945, many millions of people have been killed in over 120 wars - almost all of which were fought in the Third World. Since 1945, there has not been a single day in which one or several wars were not being fought somewhere in the world - almost all of them by weapons made in the countries of North America and Europe (East and West) and exported to the Third World.

Wars would still be possible without the international arms trade; however, they would probably be shorter and a good deal less bloody if they were not fought with advanced technology and modern weapons.

The manufacture and sale of weapons is part of a country's

preparations for war. In 'developed' countries, weapons sales are used to recoup some of the costs of re-arming with the latest weaponry. In 'developing' countries, often without their own arms industries, wars would be virtually impossible without some company or government prepared to sell the weapons needed. In time of peace, the aggressive marketing techniques can result in regional arms races; and in time of war, spare parts and weaponry are needed to keep the conflict going.

Aggressive marketing by military firms starts with massive arms fairs and travelling exhibitions, includes special government credits for sales, and goes on to bribes and 'sweeteners' offered to government officials and middlemen to win contracts. Restraints and embargoes are evaded by using faked documents and re-routing shipments through 'acceptable' countries where officials will turn a blind eye. In theory, most exporting countries do not allow trade with nations at war. In practice, blockade-running merely imposes extra costs and delays.

The recipient countries can end up in a cycle of poverty, repression and militarisation. High spending on armaments leads to a weakened economy and, in many cases, increasing reliance on international loans. Public unrest is used to justify repressive measures. The government falls more and more under the influence of the armed forces and police. The military budget continues to soar, and the cycle continues.

Helen Collinson, of the British organisation Campaign Against Arms Trade (CAAT) puts it: "The arms trade to the Third World harms millions of people, even if the weapons exported are never used. Because of their expense, arms monopolise government funds, already paltry in most Third World countries. Less money is then allocated to those items of public spending intended to meet people's basic needs such as health and education. As the arms trade has expanded, more and more wealth, resources, skills and jobs have been concentrated in the servicing of weapons rather than people".

A large proportion of the money lent to Third World governments in the 1970s was spent on arms. These purchases have generated no wealth with which to repay the loans, causing Third World countries to fall into even greater debt. The main international lending institutions, while imposing restrictions on their debtor governments' civil public spending, have made few attempts to reduce these governments' military budgets.

Repression is linked to the arms trade both directly and indirectly. Successful arms sales lead to increased military budgets, at the expense of socially-useful projects such as health, education and food, and give the army the strength to put pressure on the civilian government, and ultimately to seize power. At the same time, the military establishment acts as the friend of the rich and as a block on social reform. The result is social discontent and ferocious repression.

Over half the countries of the Third World have militarily-controlled governments. Most of these use violence against their own citizens: systematic torture, brutality, arbitrary arrest, political killings and 'disappearances'. Within non-military governments, such actions are mainly the work of the police or an out-of-control military machine.

The very tools of repression can form part of the arms trade. Computer identification systems for controlling and identifying suspects, shackles and electric-shock equipment have all been offered for sale - sometimes in the teeth of public opposition.

Exporting companies argue that, by selling arms, they provide employment for their workers and profits for their shareholders. Moral issues are not their concern, provided they meet the legal requirements. The profits are especially valuable because many weapons systems are developed for use by their own governments, which generally meet the costs of developing a new product. International sales can make it economically possible to supply a weapon for domestic use.

This financial argument is weak on two main grounds: it is not entirely true and, even if true, it is no excuse for the evil involved.

Despite appearances, arms manufacture is not a particularly good business for a worker to be in. The arms trade is unstable. Demand for weapons goes up and down unpredictably as wars start and finish and alliances are made and broken. Embargoes are imposed and lifted for political reasons. Lay-offs are frequent.

Equally, it is not a good business for a country to be in. Arms are ultimately useless when they are not lethal. To support a large export trade, a still larger internal trade in armaments is needed. The exporting country must spend more on arms than it can hope to get back in trade. High levels of spending on weaponry damage the socially-useful sectors of the economy.

Many people would also argue that they make war more likely and more devastating.

Much work has been done on the possibility of converting specific companies or districts from military to socially-useful production, in such a way that both employment and profit could be maintained. The damage done by unemployment and economic decline is real, but trading in weapons is no solution. If killing people is wrong, it is just as wrong when it is done for profit.

Economics

Tom Woodhouse

For a long time, pacifists have sought to identify the conditions of violence in the economic, social and political relationships of our society. Nuclear proliferation and the conventional arms race are seen to be symptoms of a society whose economic relationships are fundamentally based on conflict, exploitation and violence.

Wilfred Wellock, writing in *Peace News* in 1956, put the point simply and well: "Our economy is a war-producing economy. I am not interested in any disarmament policy which takes no account of basic causative factors".

In a later article, Wellock said: "The greatest benefit that would or could follow the adoption of a non-aggressive economy is the emergence of a social order of a finer culture . . . we should be able to decentralise the populations of most of our industrial cities into smallish communities . . . It is in the small community that true democracy finds its maximum opportunity".

This comment of Wellock's echoes a recurrent theme in radical and pacifist writing - the desire to establish a democratic and peaceful economy. Throughout history there has been a tension between large-scale and top-heavy forms of economic organisation on the one hand, and patterns of small-scale association on the other.

Lewis Mumford has referred to this as a conflict between two types of system: an 'authoritarian technics', centralised and powerful but inherently unstable; and a 'democratic technics', relatively weak but resourceful and durable, and based on people's skills.

The domination within the world economy, east and west, of many of the characteristics of the authoritarian technics described by Mumford has resulted in the emergence of an economy of violence, in which the following elements dominate:

• large scale production, hierarchically and bureaucratically controlled;
• high levels of conflict over possession of the world's resources, and over distribution of rewards for production;
• a complex of military interests in industry and the economy, and the domination of economic life by defence production and military research and development;
• a high demand for energy to fuel the industrial machine, and pollution and exploitation of the environment.

By contrast, a peaceful economy would have the following characteristics and principles:
• democratic control and co-operative working patterns;
• a diversity of modes of economic activity, placing primary emphasis on human-centred organisation and on meaningful work;
• security based on a conception of defence far wider than a dependence on technology (weapons);
• a regard for finite resources and the delicate balance of the environment;
• an awareness of the global consequences of economic activity.

Wilfred Wellock, who was influential in spreading Gandhi's political and economic ideas in Britain, wrote: "Western economics plundered the earth of irreplaceable resources, and violence against the earth all too easily became violence against people. A nonviolent economy would emphasise not conflict but co-operation, not conquest but harmony with nature. Gandhi called it the 'economy of permanence'. It was held together not simply by necessity and self-interest, but by mutual trust and fellowship".

Wellock influenced Ernest Bader, a Quaker businessman who wished to transform his own company into an enterprise which was closer to true Christian values. In 1951 he formed his chemicals company into the Scott Bader Commonwealth, with several key principles to guide its operation. These were that the firm should not grow beyond a limited size; that there should be a fixed ratio between the highest and lowest paid; that the members of the Commonwealth are partners and not employees; that the Board of Directors should be accountable to the Commonwealth; that the net profits should be divided between the company and the Commonwealth, 60% to the former and 40% to the latter. Half of the profits appropriated by the Commonwealth were to be paid in bonuses to members, and half to charitable purposes outside the Scott Bader organisation. The final provision was that Scott Bader Ltd should not engage in business known to be concerned with war-related purposes.

Bader and Wellock worked with Harold Farmer, a printer who had also turned his London-based business into a co-operative, to form an organisation to promote the Scott Bader principles more widely. The outcome was Demintry (the Society for Democratic Integration in Industry) which was launched in 1958. Douglas Stuckey, the treasurer of Demintry, explained the aims of the new organisation thus: "In all its activities Demintry is conscious of the imperative need to decentralise power, to operate in units small enough so that 'all those affected by a decision participate in the making of it'. It seeks to establish organic links between industry and the culture and community in which it works, using modern techniques to effect a Gandhian revolution, giving precedence to men rather than machines".

The Demintry initiative was taken at a time when the number of producers' co-operatives was at an all-time low. Growth of the new movement was slow but steady. By 1972, six companies in Britain were said to operate under the principles of the Industrial Common Ownership Movement (ICOM), as Demintry had become in 1971. By the late 1970s, up to 400 co-operatives had registered under the model rules of ICOM, and by 1985 around 1,000 co-operatives were trading.

At the same time there has been a renewal of interest in democratic economic planning, both in the labour movement and in the community more generally. The development of new technology and concern about its influence on democracy have called for a fresh assessment of the organisation of work and its relationship to the community.

There has been a change in trade union attitudes towards the role of labour in production, symbolised most of all by the campaign of the Lucas Aerospace Combine Shop Stewards' Committee and the wider workers' plans, popular planning and new technology initiatives which grew up largely under the inspiration of the Lucas model, for converting defence industries to production for peaceful purposes. Defence conversion is often seen only as a means of dealing with excess capacity in the defence industries, a means of cutting them back to suit the evolving patterns of weapons design, and to find alternative work for displaced arms workers. Peace conversion implies a broader and more imaginative vision, pointing to the need to dismantle economic conflict formations which lead to war, and to replace them with a democratic and peaceful technology.

"Peace, as has often been said, is indivisible - how then could peace be built on a foundation of reckless science and violent technology?" Schumacher's question (in *Small is Beautiful*) poses in a nutshell the importance of taking care of the economic dimension of peace. But it is heartening to conclude that, despite the visibility of the large and violent systems - tangible in weapons and wasteful technologies - there is still a flourishing sector of local skills and small-scale democratic enterprise, and a desire to sustain and develop the economy of peace.

Revolution

Mulford Sibley

Modern radicals still seem to be under the spell of violence. Although in general they may be eager to spurn it in the abstract, they are so fascinated by it that, the more imminent it becomes, the more they are willing to embrace it; or if not embrace it, at least to accept it as 'the lesser of two evils'. By and large, they still accept, even if they do not welcome, violence for 'revolutionary' ends; while they criticise those who are not revolutionists for employing it. They condemn 'reactionary' dictatorships employing violence on a large scale; but they condone, even though reluctantly, 'revolutionary' dictatorships reposing on equally great violence.

All violence tends to be 'reactionary', whatever may be the avowed objectives of those who employ it. While, in the long run, the effects of violence can no doubt be counteracted in some measure, it always leaves scars, and such progress as is made in the direction of an egalitarian society is always achieved primarily *despite* violence and not because of it.

The utilisation of violence tends to set up a kind of social logic which enhances class differentiation, promotes inequality, destroys the possibility of reconciliation and, in general, undercuts revolutionary objectives. The greater the violence, other things being equal, the less the revolution; the less the violence, again assuming equivalence of other factors, the greater the possibilities for revolution.

Violence, once employed by the alleged revolutionist, has a tendency to so enamour him of its use that he becomes unaware of other possibilities. It is so dramatic, so seemingly effective in the short run that, to the degree that it becomes a mainstay of 'revolutionary' action, the revolutionist becomes wedded to it in a kind of irrational way. Other means seem tame, slow and ineffective by comparison. The tumult, conspiratorial atmosphere and shouting, so often associated with the employment of violent means, delude the user into believing that 'something is being done' and that the opponent can be overcome only by these means.

The initial excuse for the use of violence, whether in external war or in the allegedly revolutionary situation, is that the opponent is employing it, and that one has to 'fight fire with fire'.

In the American Revolution, one finds a not dissimilar story. Initially carried on by essentially nonviolent means (at least so far as violence against persons was concerned), the obduracy and violence of the British seemed to justify the counter-violence of those who advocated independence.

The beginning phases of the Russian Revolution (whether in 1905 or in the spring of 1917) were largely nonviolent; and the Tsarist regime, like its French counterpart in the 18th century, fell with hardly the firing of a shot. Then, however, partly because of the violence of the reactionaries and partly because the Bolsheviki themselves made a cult of violence, revolutionary violence became the order of the day. The new regime of Lenin was established on the ruins of the most representative assembly ever chosen in Russian history.

The Spanish Revolution, after the overthrow of Alfonso XIII, demonstrates a similar pattern. At first largely nonviolent, it was led, after electoral reverses, to support violent revolt against a right-wing republican government. When, in turn, its exponents regained power, it was confronted with the reactionary violence of Franco's supporters. Its response was to reply violently and its justification was the usual one - the opponents of progress have turned to violence and, if we are to protect the regime, we too must use their methods.

What was the effect of 'revolutionary violence' on its users? In general, there is a very powerful case to be made for the thesis that, whenever violent methods became central, the users of violence - and those who justified it - tended to forget their original revolutionary objectives and became caught up in the imperatives of their method.

Violence demands certain things of its user: a tendency to lower the value of human life, and a gradual obscuring of ultimate ends. Although the verbal slogans may remain the same, the operative ideals of violent revolutionists become quite different. 'Victory' sets up its own imperatives which may have no necessary relationship to the proclaimed goals. Thus the really radical notions of the Declaration of Independence were transmuted into the relative conservatism of the American Constitution. The habitual use of violence by Lenin and his followers made it easy to turn their violence against former comrades like the anarchists; and the psychology of violence in the defence against Franco made it easier for the Spanish anarchists to surrender certain of their revolutionary principles.

To be sure, it was not always the literal violence which contributed to these things, but rather the contexts which appear always to accompany violence - a tendency to disregard truth, the release of destructive passions, and the ethical nihilism which seems to hover near situations in which violence is used for apparently good ends. The utilisation of violence by revolutionaries seems always to be accompanied by their absorption in the ends which violence sets up, rather than in the ends which they originally possessed.

Violence tends to force us to forget the notion of limits to human action: all methods become permissible in a situation where the opponent is destined for obliteration. If the 'logic' of violence is physical destruction of the opponent, what becomes of such demands as equality, respect for personality, and other revolutionary claims? Dead people cannot be equal, nor can their personalities be respected.

The use of violence tends to make both its wielder and its recipient unjust. The former discovers that devotion to reason is eclipsed; while the latter is tempted to retaliate in kind. Justice is incompatible with the employment of indiscriminately injurious force; whether the force be justified in the name of national defence, public order, or the revolutionary ideal of liberty, equality and fraternity.

Those who resort to violence always begin by thinking that the very threat of it will strike fear into the heart of the opponent; and that the enemy will either submit immediately or will be conquered by violent means in the name of equality. But the very nature of violence, and particularly of the organisation necessary for the revolutionary utilisation of violence, tends to take those who employ it where they do not wish to go. While it may kill reactionary enemies, it also tends to force reactionary outlooks on those who do the killing. When violence is 'successful', the surviving enemies will be suspicious, resentful and fearful. At the first opportunity, they will seek revenge.

To preserve their alleged revolutionary gains, the revolutionists will have to establish a regime of repression, belying all their claims to be egalitarians. Rigid status systems and police violence are often the fruit of violent revolution - despite the fact that it was an objective of the revolutionists to eliminate status systems and to curtail if not abolish police violence. In a very real sense, the effect of violence on the reactionary opponent is not merely to kill him but also to assure his triumph when the revolutionists claim to be successful. The reactionary has his revenge and imposes his system on the 'victor'.

Those committed to the cause of equality must cease to be attached to the romantic idealisation of violence, if they are ever to make progress in their quest. It is astonishing that so many egalitarians in the 20th century have been so impressed by the Soviet Union and Cuba, and have paid so little attention to the Scandinavian countries, where very important social changes have taken place during the past century, largely through nonviolent means. Thus many revolutionists have heard of Lenin and Castro. But how many know of the work of people like Bishop Grundtvig in 19th century Denmark, whose movement did far more to help transform a poverty-stricken, oligarchy-ruled nation than either a Lenin or a Castro did for their respective nations?

Grundtvig, however, worked with weapons of the spirit and within the context of peaceful transformation of social organisation. He had no military troops, engaged in no conspiracies, held no trials of counter-revolutionaries, armed no people's militia, issued no military manifestoes, bombed no cities, and murdered no political opponents. Yet he helped alter drastically the whole nature of the Danish society and established patterns of change that would transform political affairs as well. To be sure, Denmark has not become egalitarian in a revolutionary sense. But it is far closer to the ideal than either Cuba or the Soviet Union. And one of the reasons it is closer is because the means used have been much more nearly in accord with the ends sought than the methods employed in Cuba and Russia.

Politics

William   Hetherington

A common misconception about pacifism is that it is somehow outside politics. Pacifism *is* a political issue, because it goes to the very heart of the question as to how society is to be organised: not simply at the outward and visible level of the presence or absence of armed forces, but in the implicit assumptions about relationships between people. This means more than the basic belief that killing people is wrong. Pacifists believe that war and violence are the ultimate effects of the competitiveness and rivalries around which society, at national and international levels, has largely been structured.

For some pacifists this has resulted in a quietist attitude towards political affairs, through which some of the historic Christian peace churches, for example the Quakers and Mennonites, have at times withdrawn from mainstream political life. It was indeed a factor in some groups deciding in the 17th and 18th centuries to attempt to establish a new way of life in America.

In the 19th century a new pacifist approach to politics developed through a synthesis between pacifism and socialism. Many of those who were attracted to the socialist ideals of equality of status between human beings, regardless of class or sex, and fairer distribution of wealth and material resources amongst the whole community, were conscious that such a universal concept of social justice could not be realised without an equally universal rejection of war. In marked contrast to those on the political left who now argue that the 'armed struggle' is a necessary precondition to the achievement of social justice, for many early socialists pacifism was synonymous with their socialism.

The ideal, however, of international socialism making common nonviolent cause against capitalist or imperialist war was destroyed by the First World War. Socialists became involved in the chauvinist euphoria of both sides, and in Britain even joined the coalition government.

There were, nevertheless, other socialists who maintained the ideal of a universal 'brotherhood' (the word was not intentionally used to exclude women, since largely the same people were in the forefront of the struggle for women's rights). The significant socialist group in Britain to maintain its pacifism in this way was the Independent Labour Party, which played a notable part in anti-war and anti-conscription struggles alongside pacifists from other backgrounds.

It was still possible, because of the 'Never again' reaction of the 1930s to the carnage of the First World War, for the Labour Party itself to have pacifists as both the Leader (George Lansbury), and leader in the House of Lords (Arthur Ponsonby). But by 1935, Lansbury was ousted for his pacifism to be replaced by Clement Attlee, who was as Prime Minister to give British consent to the dropping of two atomic bombs. Since then the influence of pacifism on the Left in British politics has dwindled to negligible proportions - in parallel, perhaps, with the decline in the influence of other Christian socialist values, with which socialist pacifism was particularly linked. It was notable, indeed, that the little opposition that was shown from the Left to the Falklands War was not primarily from a pacifist perspective.

If pacifism is increasingly divorced from the Left in British politics, it has even less of a home elsewhere on the conventional political spectrum. Whereas conventional political emphasis is on who has power at the top to coerce others, pacifism derives its authority from the individual acting ultimately on personal responsibility. Pacifists refuse to accept that the mere accident of being born in Britain involves a duty to obey the order of a 'British government' to kill other human beings who happen to have been born elsewhere.

A major distinction between a pacifist approach to political affairs and that of the major political parties is the pacifist emphasis on the relationship between ends and means. Aldous Huxley, pacifist and novelist, commented on international politics as war loomed again in 1937, "We go on believing, against all the evidence, that bad means can achieve the good ends we desire".

Another way of putting it is that pacifism applies the principles of individual morality to the problems of politics and economics. Militarism by its nature justifies assault and murder at the state level but prohibits such crimes to the private citizen. Pacifism rejects such a double standard of morality: If it is wrong for the individual to kill or injure for personal reasons, it is equally wrong to kill or injure for political ends.

Pacifists believe that if we want a peaceful, free and just world for the whole of humanity, then we can bring it about only by acting, not simply individually but also collectively, in a peaceful, free and just way. Many pacifists use the term 'nonviolent revolution' for such a gradual ongoing process, in contrast to the conventional political concept of a revolution as an immediate bloody uprising, a seizing of power by militaries or paramilitaries. As Bart de Ligt, an influential pacifist writer, said, "The more violence, the less revolution". The real revolution, in the sense of a lasting transformation of society rather than the displacement of one autocracy by another, comes about through individuals nonviolently taking control over their own lives. No pacifist pretends that this is easy. It was Huxley again who wrote: "If one wants peace, one must care for those things which make for peace - care for them to the point of actually putting oneself to considerable personal inconvenience".

Such personal inconvenience may take the form of the loss of freedom, status or income that arises from refusing military service, rejecting work in military-related industry, or resisting the payment of war taxes. It may mean much patient explaining to shops and manufacturers why one finds their military-orientated products or advertising offensive. On the other hand, one may have to start thinking for oneself instead of leaving large decisions to government, and to take account of the needs of other people in a spirit of co-operation and caring rather than competition and selfishness.

It is not enough for pacifists to prefer democracy to dictatorship, because it is by no means certain that democracy presently works towards a more peaceful world. Democracy can in practice be the tyranny of the supposed majority. It is seriously to be questioned whether in ultimate issues the 'will of the majority' has any inherent moral virtue.

Instead, many pacifists are interested in consensus decision-making - a method highly developed by Quakers but also increasingly used by radical peace groups. Under this system, a difficult issue is not dealt with by a confrontational debate which polarises divisions, leading to a vote which may well leave the minority frustrated. The whole group enters the debate with a prior commitment to achieving consensus - a general agreement of the whole body. This necessarily requires much patience and persistence, particularly in listening to what others are saying, and the attempt is not always successful. It is felt that this is the most likely way to achieve decisions which people are happy to support because they have directly contributed to their making.

Such a system cannot easily be translated to the decision-making involved in elections, but it follows that pacifists would generally prefer systems of proportional representation to a 'winner takes all' system. It is indeed the concept of 'winning' with its counterpart of 'losing', that pacifists are concerned to change.

For pacifists there is a much closer relationship between the personal and the political than conventional politicians would admit. So much of politics is about coercing people to conform to the state - be it ever so democratic. Pacifism means creating a society in which humans can be human. Through it all runs the continuing refrain, ''If you want peace, prepare for peace''.

Anarchism

Ronald Sampson

The conventional view of anarchy is very simple. Anarchy means absence of government; government is necessary to maintain law and order; without law and order, life is hell for everybody. Therefore, government is good and anarchy is bad. All decent people can understand propositions so simple and self-evident; therefore, people who actually advocate anarchy must be either wicked or unbalanced.

The conventional, seemingly plausible view is nevertheless incorrect. The connection between anarchism and pacifism is very close, and I propose to commence with pacifism.

Pacifists are people who refuse under any circumstances to be a party to the shedding of human blood. A characteristic slogan summarises the pacifist conviction: ''Wars will cease when men refuse to fight'' - and only when men refuse to fight. Pacifists accordingly declare in advance their solemn intention not to fight and invite you, non-pacifists, to join them. The logic is impeccable. But the wars go on just the same; moreover, they get worse.

So the pacifist must ask why this rational remedy is not producing the desired results. ''Come and join us'', the pacifists say, but they appeal in vain. Is it not odd? Virtually nobody wants war; why then do people prefer so stubbornly to reject the pacifists' self-evident solution?

Wars do not happen out of the blue - ever! It is not possible, simply because they require too much advance preparation. They are always preceded by a state of armed preparation. Why? One of the most urgent tasks is to illuminate public opinion at least sufficiently to make it impossible for Ministers of Armaments any longer to masquerade under the cloak of ''Defence''.

The reservoir of armed violence (as large and destructive as every government can possibly afford), permanently on tap, is necessary because without it a government would be at a disadvantage *vis à vis* other governments, whose armoured reservoirs it does not (as yet) control. Disadvantaged in what respect? In the matter of control over wealth, people, natural resources, that is to say, power. Governments themselves pretend that they innocently seek no more than an equilibrium; but the falsity of this claim is evidenced by the fact that equilibrium could be maintained at the level of one soldier each, and this kind of equilibrium never exists. Moreover, the allegedly sought-after equilibrium has always erupted in war and must always do so, because the reality is a struggle for power, that is to say, domination.

Government results not from the welfare necessities of people inherent in their God-given or biological situation; but it results from the all-consuming, devouring determination of some individuals to obtain, consolidate and, if possible, expand their power over their fellows.

Nothing can ever legitimise this state of affairs for two simple reasons: firstly, the terrible consequences that ensue from this theory for humankind as a whole in the shape of ceaselessly recurring war; and secondly, because human beings are in fact in all essentials equal, and it is a violation of God's will that some people should be subjected to the power and domination of other people, when all people are alike God's creatures, subject in common not to other people like themselves but to God alone.

Power by definition means the ability to force someone to do that which they would not do of their own free will, and it is precisely this that is not justifiable. It is from this element of force, of coercion, that all the resentment and counter-irritants and desire for vengeance, in short, evil, are triggered off. It is previous power - a legacy of countless acts of power - that has made the present oppressor or aggressor what he is; and more power can only add to the evil ingredients of the existing situation. The only reply to power and its evil consequences is not counter-power, which is simply more power, but *anti-power*, which is the opposite of power, namely courageous, unyielding powerlessness, or love.

Violence itself is the outcome of the will to power in man. Chairman Mao was undoubtedly right when he observed that "political power flows out of the barrel of a gun", but he forgot to add the even more important converse of the proposition, namely that the barrel of a gun flows from the will to power. It is this will to power itself which is the source of most of the evils which threaten to overwhelm us.

To abstain, therefore, from the quest for power is logically entailed by an understanding of the evil of violence. To renounce power means abandoning all idea of getting power, of seeking to overthrow the rulers, of bringing about a revolution, of devising blueprints for new institutions. In their stead, anarchists seek to eradicate the evil potentialities in themselves and, by so doing, to change the nature of their relations with other people. When enough people succeed in doing this, the social institutions which reflect existing human beliefs and relations, will of necessity begin to change.

Feminism

Rachel Hope

Since pacifists pledge themselves to resist all forms of oppression, there should be a keen awareness amongst them with regard to one of the most fundamental oppressions - that of women by men. It has led to male domination of the family, of politics and of culture itself, thereby ensuring the continuation of a patriarchy which has been in existence in Western society since history was first recorded.

Feminism, in broad terms, is the struggle against this domination. While there is a long history of women's involvement and achievements in the peace movement since the turn of the century, during the last twenty years the advocates of the rights of women in social, political and economic spheres have had some successes. This essay looks briefly at two issues central to feminism, and at pacifism's response to these: firstly, the struggle against institutional power which has been shaped and is maintained by men, and secondly, feminist concern with individual male violence. (The use of 'men' and 'women' does not imply a generalisation about either sex but refers to culturally defined groups.)

Firstly, the domination of women by men is a constant feature in all societies' structures. For example, the nation state as an institution exists to preserve certain social, economic and political relations within its borders. These relations will ensure continued male supremacy, as it is mainly men who control them for the benefit of themselves and other men. The state uses bureaucracy to inhibit direct communication between those in power and others, including women, who try to make their voices heard. It will use violence, or the threat of violence through repressive legislation and other means, to maintain control. Capitalism likewise ensures economic dominance for men, as they buy and sell labour like any other commodity. The aim of capitalism is profit and wealth for the few, so exploitation akin to violence is experienced by the majority of the population at every stage - from the production of raw materials, for example, by women workers in the Third World receiving a pittance for growing cash crops, to factory workers enduring poor pay and conditions.

Vital to the maintenance of state and capitalism is another institution - the armed forces. The army is there to defend us from outside enemies, we are told and - we can assume - from elements within society which threaten cultural values.

However since many, including many women, do not benefit fully from the society which men have created, feminists see the value of the armed forces as questionable. The war machine is undoubtedly a male preserve. Recruitment advertisements until recently spelled out ''it's a man's life in the army'', and today the appeal is couched in terms specific to characteristics associated with men, such as toughness, aggression, competitiveness. Pacifists are glad that few feminists are taken in by some armies' claim in recent years to be 'equal opportunity' employers, as the armed forces look to women to swell their ranks.

Feminists have pointed also to the violence emanating from men's desire for power, within the institution of today's nuclear family. Women generally become socially and economically dependent on their husbands, particularly when they have children. Women are chiefly responsible for childcare, yet they receive little recognition for it either from society or within the family where the father is seen as the chief figure of authority.

This leads to the second tenet of feminism to be discussed - women's concern with individual male violence. Feminists believe that male violence has its roots in the structures outlined above, but have also developed strategies for dealing with the practicalities of abuse by men towards women. Pacifists too are committed to resisting such violence, and their methods of doing so reflect the needs and philosophy of many feminists. The worth of each individual is a concept basic to feminism; as also are individual responsibility and the belief that every person has some measure of personal influence in every situation, however oppressed that person may be. Women have always been trained to be passive but, with feminist insight, many women have shown enormous strength in their refusal to submit to battering and rape by men known and not known to them. Some have worked at great personal cost to support other women who have not been able to free themselves from violent situations. As a pacifist one could wish that feminist techniques for dealing with male aggression were always nonviolent, but this will not be possible until women are confident enough of themselves and each other to fully explore such methods. Though pacifists affirm the Gandhian view of the positive value of self-sacrifice and suffering, we need to be aware of the voice of women, who will not be victims, and who will suffer no longer.

Solidarity among women has long been considered a threat by men. Feminism's unashamed insistence on putting women first has been viewed with suspicion by some pacifists who say that this is divisive and that it is wrong for women to organise separately. It is not the expectation of women generally that roles should be reversed and that men should suffer domination and exclusion as women have done. Rather women would hope that a genuine position of equality be reached; but they maintain that it is up to men to make thorough changes in their behaviour and in their situations which will benefit themselves and at the same time not exploit women.

The image which feminists have in the eyes of the public is not a pacifist one. It is ironic that the peace movement and all those who are working for radical change could benefit from those qualities often present in women, which men have taken for granted, and used to their own advantage. These include displaying sensitivity and a caring attitude towards others at all times, and having the capability to comfort and support, whatever they may be feeling themselves. In spite of their traditional image as 'conciliators', pacifists should learn to exploit the strong feelings of love and anger, the hatred of oppression and injustice, and to face up to fear in real action, just as feminists are succeeding in expressing such feelings in spite of women's traditional image as the 'gentler' sex.

Human Rights

Jan Melichar

"Everyone has the right to life, liberty and security of person".

This is the third article of the United Nations' Universal Declaration of Human Rights, which was agreed in 1948. Forty-eight nations voted in favour, eight abstained. There were no dissensions.

The right to life is a right without which all other rights can have no meaning. To take someone's life, to kill someone, is to strip them of all their rights. Yet it is the right which even the most liberal opinion is willing to abandon. It is argued that, to defend liberty or gain freedom, the right to life must take a back seat.

This ambiguity which has been deeply embedded in religious, political and economic institutions for centuries, is one of the prime reasons for the schizophrenic state of the world. Simultaneously to value something and be prepared to destroy it leads to confusion and madness. In physical terms, this ambiguity has led to an ever-increasing destruction of human life - over 180 million killed this century in wars; to a political and economic order which, at best, turns a blind eye to the suffering and death of countless millions and at worst is underpinned by it. Killing is the final exploitation.

Human rights are of course not carved on some cosmic tablet, ageless and perpetual; they are a fairly recent invention. The concept originates in Greco-Roman natural law, which held that human conduct should be judged according to the law of nature. However, the concern here was with duties rather than rights, and it embraced slavery. Between the Renaissance and the 17th century, such things as the Magna Carta and the English Bill of Rights shifted the ground and viewed human beings as endowed with certain eternal rights.

The conception of natural rights and laws was elaborated by people such as Rousseau, and further advanced by the struggle against political absolutism in the late 18th and 19th century. It is these arguments that are still central today. Natural law as the foundation of human rights was continually under attack until the 20th century when, following the Second World War and the foundation of the United Nations, human rights were given a new lease of life.

Now the existence of human rights is no longer debated, and the Universal Declaration of Human Rights represents commonly-agreed guidelines for human relationships - a manifesto with primary moral authority. However, there are problems with such a manifesto, as indeed with any moral statement. Even tyrants like to say that they have right or God on their side, and governments like to have rights too.

Following the acceptance of the UNDHR, additional covenants have added legal force to it. In certain respects these covenants have transmuted, indeed negated, the third and most fundamental article. "In time of public emergency . . . the State Parties . . . may take measures derogating from their obligations". And "Every human being has the inherent right to life. This right shall be protected by *law*. No one shall be *arbitrarily* deprived of his life", but "sentence of death may be imposed only for most serious crimes in accordance with the *law* in force".

The European Convention on Human Rights, formulated some years later, is a lot plainer on this issue. It "transformed fifteen of the principles proclaimed by the United Nations (Universal Declaration) into legal obligations, which thus guarantee the fundamental civil and political rights of Man".

Article 2

1. Everyone's right to life shall be protected by *law*. No one shall be deprived of his life intentionally *save* in the execution of a sentence of a court following his conviction of a crime for which the *penalty is provided by law*.

2. Deprivation of life shall not be regarded as inflicted in contravention of this Article when it results from the use of force which is no more than absolutely necessary:

(a) in defence of any person from *unlawful* violence;

(b) in order to effect *lawful* arrest or to prevent the escape of a person lawfully detained;

(c) in action *lawfully* taken for the purpose of quelling a riot or insurrection.

Article 15

In time of *war or other public emergency threatening the life of the nation, any High Contracting Parties may take measures derogating from its obligations.*

These legal instruments, we can see, are a long way removed from the original declaration "Everyone has the right to life . . . " What has happened is that the State has become a special entity with rights of its own and with the additional and exclusive right to kill - that is, to remove the basis of all human rights. The primacy of the State over the individual is thus disguised as 'human rights'.

Here lies the biggest challenge to all those concerned with human rights and to all of us as individuals. Are we willing for the State to have control over life and death? Are we willing to take the risk to challenge and dismantle the State's ability and power to wage war? Are we willing to take the risk of exploring and building new and humane relationships between people, where human rights will mean just that, and not simply rights for oneself at other people's cost?

For pacifists this is the central issue and the basic principle from which all else flows. The pacifist's focus on war is a focus on the abuse of the most fundamental human right, and it is an active resistance to all institutions, social and political systems which perpetuate this abuse, and an active search for a more human social order.

Law and Order

William   Hetherington

It is natural that pacifists extend their total rejection of war and militarism to the wider context of how society must be re-ordered to minimise organised violence in any form. This brings them immediately to the penal process. After war, the gravest manifestation of legalised violence in any country is the punishment of crime; not only the hangings, the beheadings, the burnings and gassings; not only the tortures and maimings, the whippings and beatings, but also the imprisonments, the exiles, the humiliations and separations of people from ordinary human contacts.

Pacifists do not have a common critique of crime comparable to that of war. One of the basic distinctions, however, between the traditional approach to crime and that of the exponent of nonviolence is the difference between the belief that aggression and violence are inherent in mankind, so that people must be restrained by authority, and the belief that love and co-operation are the original human qualities which society has too often warped. Enthusiasts for 'law and order' argue that humans are so intent upon murder, rape and pillage that only a deterrent penal system will keep them in check. Pacifists are inclined to believe that, left to themselves, humans have a capacity for mutual caring, tolerance and forgiveness which the penal system often leaves out of account.

There is the classic paradox of locking up both the murderer for killing and the conscientious objector for refusing to kill. The former, of whom it has been said that murder is a mere incident in a miserable life, is ostracised. The war machine that encompasses the death of us all is glorified. Again, if, as Dwight Eisenhower once said, "every bomb that is built is a theft from those who are hungry", what moral right have the states who build those bombs to accuse those who help themselves to a little of the wealth of which they have been dispossesed? If killing and stealing are indeed wrong, then they are as wrong for organised society as for the individual.

The continuing debate over capital punishment presents the issue of violent or nonviolent remedies in its starkest form. Supporters of capital punishment have even argued that execution is valid as a 'deterrent'. For pacifists, execution both degrades society to the level of murder itself and negates any possibility of repentance or reformation. It follows that pacifists also reject all forms of physical violence and torture, either for punishment or to extract confessions.

Imprisonment, however, is a more complex issue. It can be said that any form of imprisonment is a form of 'structural violence'. On the other hand, it may be argued that, in our present imperfect state of society, some form of containment must be provided for seriously violent offenders. This need not negate two basic principles. One is that people are sent to prison as a punishment and not for punishment. The deprivation of liberty is the sanction, rather than the inhumane conditions of overcrowding, lack of sanitation, and enforced idleness - which 'law and order' enthusiasts often demand to be made more harsh. The other principle is that, even if imprisonment may be necessary for seriously violent offenders, it is in no way a constructive solution for the thousands of petty offenders who are now gaoled. Sending such people to prison is not only extremely costly of society's resources, but also counter-productive because it confirms such people's own sense of worthlessness and rejection by society, so leading to the repeated pattern of offence-imprisonment-offence.

Pacifists have made a notable contribution to such penal reform in Britain as the abolition of capital and corporal punishment, the betterment of prison regimes and the introduction of the probation system. In some cases the motivation towards reform has come as a direct result of experience of the penal system arising from pacifist activity. Similar experience of the trial process has not yet led to notable reform. Indeed, articulate defendants often perceive that there is a sense of conveyor-belt justice for most of those who appear before a magistrate's court.

Before punishment or even trial, one encounters the police. It used to be the proud boast of Britain that, unlike those in most other countries, our police were essentially civilian and unarmed. In recent years, we have seen an increasing militarisation and arming of the police. It is significant that, just as the Special Branch (the political police) was founded to deal with the Irish problem of the 19th century, so the increasing militarisation of the police has been largely in relation to the 20th-century 'troubles'. The 'riot gear' of shields, visors and heavy truncheons which first appeared in Northern Ireland, spread like a rash across Britain during the 1984 miners' strike. Plastic bullets and CS gas have followed, making the police on some occasions indistinguishable from the army, yet answerable only to themselves.

If truth is the touchstone of justice, it is also in Gandhian terms the touchstone of nonviolence. Nowhere are the thoughts expressed in this article more appropriately summed up than in the words of Oscar Wilde, himself imprisoned for a 'crime' we no longer recognise:

I know not whether laws be right
Or whether laws be wrong.
All that we know who lie in gaol
Is that the walls are strong . . .
That every prison that men build
Is built with bricks of shame
And bound with bars, lest Christ should see
How men their brothers maim.

Racism

James Gordon

Jesus preached non-resistance in the face of oppression or evil, and his philosophy quite clearly implied condemnation of the view that some people are superior to others by accidents of birth or background. Indeed, some of his strongest recorded words were directed at those of his own religion and race who set themselves up above others just because of 'whose sons' they were. In our own era, both Martin Luther King and Mahatma Gandhi adopted a philosophy and practice of nonviolence in action which demonstrated that pacifism and campaigning for racial and other equalities go hand in hand.

King was concerned to liberate the Black community in the United States, Gandhi to liberate subject peoples in India (and earlier in South Africa). Both deliberately chose the method of nonviolence as the *most effective* means of attaining their objectives, as well as the most morally defensible. In both cases, there were those of their followers who advocated violence, and who have since claimed that their espousal of violent methods was more effective than these apostles and practitioners of nonviolence.

The examples of Christ, King and Gandhi all exemplify that pacifism is no soft option. All suffered, physically and mentally; all were finally murdered.

Jesus' famous words ''by their fruits you shall know them'' is an appropriate test of those professing pacifism, as it is of those professing anti-racism. Just holding pacifist or anti-racist views is not enough. You must speak out, or indeed act out. King and Gandhi both inspired mass-movements which were effective in significantly changing the power relations in their societies in their own lifetimes. King had a major effect in advancing the cause of Black people in American society, while Gandhi and his followers showed the British they had no right, moral or otherwise, to rule India. King and Gandhi used every device in the book except violence, and they used them with intelligence and skill to change perceptions and practice, and thus to change the face of history.

Jesse Jackson, a disciple of King and now a contender for political power in the USA, earlier ran a campaign telling Black people: "You are somebody". King's mass demonstrations included Black people simply standing with placards round their necks which read: "I am a man". These are two examples of effective nonviolent strategies against racism. Both struck at the heart of the racist ideology which regards one group of people as inferior, less intelligent, or just less worthy than the group to which the adherent of the ideology belongs. This ideology can be expressed in forms that are comparatively petty, such as verbal abuse, or in forms that are abominable. Whether the group is merely abused and degraded or subjected to violence, torture or death, the racism is always based in a fundamental denial of full humanity.

In the USA and in Britain, there have been real attempts to tackle racism in society through campaigns, public education and use of the law. While these efforts are a long way in both societies from bringing complete equality between Black and White people, it is worth noting that they are very largely nonviolent in character.

At first sight, the South African case may seem to support the view that there is a point when pacifism as a strategy has to give way to one involving the use of violence. The African National Congress under Nelson Mandela was originally nonviolent, but was pushed by various provocations from the South African Whites to take up violent forms of resistance. Many pacifists might understand them but will argue that the role of such nonviolent people as Desmond Tutu and Alan Boesak has been crucial in harnessing the sympathy of the powers that have been successful in pressuring South Africa towards change. There will always be an argument about whose strategy was the more effective. Certainly the use and advocacy of violence by an oppressed person can always be used to legitimise the use of coercion by the oppressor, who usually has access to resources such as control of the media, and can use them to valuable effect.

One can understand those who feel driven to violence by the outrage of racism. But nonviolence has played a part, often much uncredited, in shifting attitudes and sympathies. Determination to treat the oppressor as a fellow human being, despite his or her degrading or worse treatment of you, has always been a feature of the best nonviolent action. And it has had some remarkable successes.

No state can ever totally ignore public opinion. Actions designed to teach the public about the inhumanity of state policies towards particular groups of people always stand a chance of being effective, even if their effect is not felt immediately. The more costly that teaching is to the teacher, the more likely it is to arouse sympathy - and thus affect opinion and practice. An armchair or purely negative pacifism, a pacifism that will not risk, will not go out and confront the evil directly in both word and action, is not just a flawed pacifism, but is ultimately no pacifism at all.

The Environment and the Green Movement

Ian Davis

"When you have cut down the last tree and polluted the last river, you will know that you cannot eat money". - Chief Seattle, c1855.

Ever since I first read this native American saying, it has stuck in my mind as the grimmest of prophecies. Despite the massive increase in material output in the last hundred years, large sections of the world's people are poorer in many ways. The world is more crowded, more polluted, less stable ecologically and - having opened the nuclear Pandora's Box - we move closer each day to Armageddon.

But increasingly the fear of nuclear war is being obscured by ecological spectres. Even the most 'advanced' industrial societies cannot hide from the cumulative effects of the present ecological crises. Contaminated water supplies, deforestation, desertification, loss of species and habitat, holes in the ozone layer, acid rain and the greenhouse effect represent a common danger that no nation can afford to ignore.

The rapid growth of green ideas in the 1980s has arisen from the failure of the Old Order - both capitalist and socialist - to provide meaningful and sustainable solutions to these global problems. Even more significant, perhaps, is the charge against the Old Order of complicity in nurturing this common threat.

In attempting to articulate a new vision for humankind, I shall argue that Greens and Pacifists are natural allies. It is surely anachronistic for those who are worried about militarism, those who are concerned about poverty and hunger, and those who are anxious for the environment, to work in isolation from each other. The common threat can only be averted by a common and co-operative response. In today's globally warmed climate, an environmentally unfriendly pacifist is a contradiction in terms.

The word 'green' is used in many different contexts by many different people. For most people, 'green' simply means 'the environment', but there is much more to the green agenda than narrow environmental issues. Jonathon Porritt has described the Green Movement as "the most dynamic social and political movement since the birth of socialism". It is salutary to remember, however, that we are talking about a movement that is still in its infancy.

The diversity of the Green Movement and its ability to attract a wide variety of people is, I think, a source of great strength. While the search for a common perspective can be likened to the search for that elusive pot of gold at the end of the rainbow, I see the following as key green principles:
· ecological wisdom;
· respect for the dignity of every human being;
· internationalism;
· an economic system that is decentralised and equitable;
· grassroots democracy and nonviolence at all levels of society.

I would venture to suggest that these are also the key components in pacifist thought.

Perhaps the major thread linking pacifism and green thought is the shared belief in the need to closely associate means and ends. I firmly believe that the means chosen to achieve social change directly determine the structure of the subsequent society. "Acts of violence", said Gandhi, "create bitterness in the survivors and brutality in the destroyers". Thus the nonviolent transformation of society can be the only true path for Greens and Pacifists alike.

As a self-proclaimed green pacifist, how does my commitment to peace equate with my desire for social change? In coming to terms with such a dilemma, I keep in mind a positive conception of peace. Rather than simply taking peace to mean the absence of war, I regard peace as a process in which all people are helped to develop to their full potential. Clearly, the majority of the world's population are being prevented - by conditions of social injustice, economic exploitation and political oppression - from reaching anywhere near their full potential. Indeed, this 'structural violence' maintains the social and economic order in which we live. It also condemns millions of people to lives of poverty and misery.

The foremost task of the green pacifist should be to denounce the structural violence on which the present system is based and pursue ways of transforming the situation without violence. We must make other peace campaigners aware of the integral link between modern industrial societies and the probability of violence and war.

"Militarism", according to R H Tawney, "is the characteristic, not of an army, but of a society". Similarly, structural violence is the characteristic, not of a particular political ideology, but of all modern industrial societies in which the maximisation of material output is seen as the primary means of meeting people's needs. Adam Smith and Karl Marx are part of the same problem - both sustain the myth that infinite growth is possible (and desirable) from the Earth's finite resources.

Were Chief Seattle alive today, I am certain that he would agree with Jeremy Seabrook when he says that "money cannot cure what money has caused". To check the destructive momentum of economic growth requires the ascendancy of humanitarian values over material values. This will inevitably mean fundamental changes in the way we live our lives; a switch in emphasis from consumption to conservation. But in an age of modern communications and technology, it is comforting to know that radical ideas and examples can circulate around the world as fast as money. The principal idea and example of green pacifists - "protect the Earth and we protect ourselves" and "live simply so that others may simply live" - build upon the Gandhian non-violent tradition which has already spanned the world.

Organic Peace

Kim Taplin

My brief is to say something about pacifism in relation to the environment. I need to start by firmly laying claim to the idea that peace is something that needs to be made, rather than something that exists as long as we don't protest. The liturgy of the Anglican Church contains the exhortation "Let us pursue all that makes for peace and builds up our common life". It is a sentence that I find both deep and satisfying, and I do not think it is necessary to be a Christian to share the desire and intention it affirms. The verbs 'pursue' and 'build up' set forth a vision of peacemaking that is active and constructive.

Let me now turn to the other half of my subject and ask what is meant by the environment. Psychologists debate the relative importance of heredity and environment in the formation of human character. In that sense, though a very personal thing, environment is at the same time widely inclusive - being no less than the total situation in which, complete with your fixed inheritance of genes, you wake to find yourself. It can be modified; though we have always been a lot less clear than other species about what kind of environment we find most favourable to our optimum development: spiritual, physical and mental. I would suggest one in which a rich and positive peace is under construction as good for all three.

It is wise to bear this in mind when we consider the environment of which these days we speak most often and most anxiously; and by which we seem to mean three of what the ancients called the Four Elements - earth, air and water. These, as most of us are by now aware, we have recently been more and more rapidly poisoning. In the process we have wiped out some species entirely, while many others are under threat. Many of our own species have a wretched quality of life and meet an untimely death because of our bad management of the environment.

As a Christian, I prefer to use the word Creation. The word implies tending and nurturing, rather than adjusting. It speaks of love given and love asked for. I offer the word humbly, in the knowledge that it will put some people off. Though so does the word environment. There is a coldness about its connotations that makes us feel rather helpless. We may - we should! - be conscientiously turning off lights, using ecological cleaning products and unleaded petrol, buying or growing organic food, and so on. However we are still involved despite ourselves, in a daily web of compromises; things we cannot avoid if we live as part of normal Western Society and which, even if we devote ourselves to some radically alternative way of living, we cannot avoid altogether. Such considerations depress a well-meaning person as much as the thought of what others, who are less aware and less well-meaning, are doing to earth, air and water by the way *they* live.

Perhaps a helpful idea is that of the Given. This has the advantage of throwing a kind of bridge between the perceptions of science and religion. It contains the idea of Gift, or something freely and lovingly offered and to be valued. Yet it also contains the scientific notion of Data, the given, irreducible facts with which we have to work. In fact, it marries fact and value, and shows that they are one flesh.

The Given is the given for all of us, all human beings and all creatures great and small. The Judaeo-Christian tradition has been accused - I think a little unjustly - of inculcating a cavalier attitude to Nature in the past. St Francis is one of many who might be set in the other scale. This is not the place to go into that debate, but it is certainly important to note that more influential voices are now being raised everyday to help build up a Creation-centred theology that points to environmental issues as being a central place for the exercise of Christian responsibility and love of neighbour. The planet is forcing us to realise at last that we are siblings; in beginning to make peace with Nature, we learn that we have common interests and must make peace with each other.

When Shakespeare's Macbeth became embroiled in evil because of his "vaulting ambition", it is highly significant that he became careless of the consequences not only to other people but to the whole of nature. He questions the powers of darkness and is prepared for the price of an answer to be a long list of natural calamities, culminating in

> . . . though the treasure
> Of Nature's germens tumble all together
> Even till destruction sicken . . .

In other words, his individual craving is to be satisfied even if it leads to ecological disaster. And of course he will remain unsatisfied in any case, because nothing that is divisive and destructive does satisfy our deepest needs. Shakespeare's wide-ranging wisdom points to the perennial truth concerning our 20th-century situation: that those who are divided against themselves will soon be divided against their fellows and, thence in an unholy declension of increasing recklessness, will be implicated in the confounding of the whole ecosphere. The alternative is a peace that builds outwards from the attempt to heal inner divisions, towards neighbours, towards nations, and finally to Nature itself.

Christianity

Alan Litherland

Christian pacifism has its roots in the life, teaching and death of
Jesus. Much of the Old Testament saw God as a "Lord of armies"
who often supported and directed the wars of Israel, but Jesus
by his actions identified himself with two quite different Old
Testament concepts. By riding into Jerusalem on an ass, the
symbol of work and peace, he symbolically lived out the prophet
Zechariah's vision (Zech 9:9) of a Messiah who would banish
chariots and war-horses and "speak peaceably to every nation".
In the "temptations" at the start of his ministry he rejected the
Devil's offer of help in winning over "the nations of the world",
and it later became apparent that he chose instead the way of the
Cross, taking the part of the suffering servant of the second
Isaiah (Isaiah 53) who would redeem humanity by his own
undeserved suffering.

At a time when Israel, an occupied country, was seething with
revolt, he carefully avoided identification with the revolutionary
Zealots, and foresaw (Luke 19:41) that armed rebellion against
Rome would bring, not liberation, but destruction - "and not
leave you one stone standing on another". The rebellion finally
took place in AD 66, Jerusalem was destroyed and the Jewish
nation ceased to exist.

The key words of his teaching were faith, love and forgiveness. In this context, 'love' is not a sentiment but a way of treating
other people, an active benevolence which ignores man-made
barriers of class or nation. In the sermon on the mount he taught
his followers to love their enemies and respond to evil with good,
to aggression with nonviolence.

This teaching was addressed to ordinary people, not politicians, and was primarily concerned with personal relationships.
There was no direct guidance in the New Testament on
whether, or to what extent, the same ethic should govern the

behaviour of nations. Is a double standard permissible - love, compassion and forgiveness for individuals in personal relationships; but terror, killing and destruction for a nation at war? Christian pacifists find this inconceivable. Although the decision to use armed force in war is usually a collective decision, it is implemented by individuals. It is what people do to people that counts - killing, maiming, burning and starving people on the other side until they submit. It is those actions which have to be set against the standard of Christ's life and teaching, not the alleged aims for which a war is fought.

The early Church took the teaching of Jesus literally, and for nearly 300 years Christian leaders unequivocally opposed violence and killing for any purpose. They did not develop any sophisticated theology of pacifism, but quoted a few simple texts in support of their stand. As Christianity became more influential, however, and Christians became involved in affairs of state, attitudes changed. When Constantine became Emperor, he made Christianity the official religion of the Roman Empire. The Church turned from its original pacifism and accepted the use of armed force by the state as justifiable.

Individual statements re-stating the old, uncompromising rejection of war are recorded for some time after that, and much later minority Christian sects returned to a way of life based on a more literal interpretation of the Lord's teaching, adopting the pacifist position of the early Church: the Cathars in the ninth century, Waldenses in the twelfth, Anabaptists and Mennonites in the sixteenth, Quakers in the seventeenth, and so on. The main stream of Christian thought, however, was and still is equivocal.

Now in the nuclear age, more and more Christians are concerned about the right response to violence and war, and a statement by the 1978 Lambeth Conference of Anglican bishops described the use of the modern technology of war as "the most striking example of corporate sin and the prostitution of God's gifts", but those who accept the full pacifist position are still in a small minority. They do so, mainly, not on the basis of a few proof texts, but from a consideration of the whole tenor of Jesus's life, teaching and death on the cross.

The Cross has always been central to the Christian faith, and is regarded as a demonstration of God's way of dealing with evil in man. Jesus called his followers to "take up their cross" and follow his example of love. The use of mass killing, or the threat of mass killing, to deal with communism, or the invasion of islands in the South Atlantic, or the oppression of a dictatorial government, is the opposite of the Christian approach and a denial of the Christian faith. In biblical terms, it is the blasphemy of worshipping the Devil, by accepting that only his methods will work in God's world. The pacifist alternative to power politics is to create conditions for justice, to devote resources to meeting human need instead of stockpiling weapons of destruction, to respect and trust peoples of other nations, to build bridges of reconciliation, to develop nonviolent ways of resisting aggression or oppression. All these are consistent with Christ's way and could be called the corporate equivalent, in practical terms, of his teaching on individual relationships.

Most Christians would accept most of these positive steps, and mainstream Christian thinking is moving slowly towards the pacifist position, though the great majority, in spite of all the moral arguments, still find it difficult to accept the apparent defencelessness which the pacifist position implies. The Christian pacifist attitude to violence was eloquently expressed by Pope John Paul II in his 1979 sermon at Drogheda, though he does not seem to regard himself as a pacifist: "Violence is a lie, for it goes against the truth of our faith, the truth of our humanity. Violence destroys what it claims to defend: the dignity, the life, the freedom of human beings. Violence is a crime against humanity, for it destroys the very fabric of society. . . .

"To all of you who are listening I say: do not believe in violence; do not support violence. It is not the Christian way. It is not the way of the Catholic Church. Believe in peace and forgiveness and love, for they are of Christ."

Buddhism

Christopher Titmuss

Buddhism might be regarded as the collective effort to keep alive the 2,500 year-old teachings of the Buddha. The word 'Buddhism' is a generalised western concept, used originally by western scholars, to summarise a wide body of spiritual teachings on awakening, which have influenced a diversity of cultures. Through the centuries, the person of Gautama Siddharta, known as the Buddha, inspired further awakening among the community of meditators, with the themes of nonviolence, compassionate action and wise attention standing firm.

The Buddha has remained a constant reminder of the necessity to safeguard a nonviolent approach to dealing with threatening and painful circumstances, rather than resorting to violence. He teaches pacifism without being passive. The Buddha has described his teachings as consisting of a three-fold practice (*sikha*): namely ethics (*sila*), meditative awareness (*samadhi*) and wisdom (*panna*).

Ethics consist of the undertaking to refrain from killing, stealing, sexual abuse, lying and substance-abuse that disturbs the clarity of mind.

In other words, the first teaching principle of the Buddha is the commitment to nonviolence. In its most simple interpretation this means simply not killing another human being under any circumstances. But the principle is used by the Buddha to establish a set of social relationships in which all people are worthy of being treated with respect, since all are exposed to birth, ageing, pain and death.

In different passages, he returned again and again to the theme of nonviolence. "Hatred does not cease by hatred. Hatred ceases only by love. This is the eternal law". He places much emphasis on the inter-connectedness of human life and faith in humanity. He refused to accept any kind of penal code in the way of capital or corporal punishment, lashings, severance of limbs or appeals to revenge. "Those who harbour revenge cannot be free from hatred".

The Buddha established the *sangha* (it literally means 'gathering'). The *sangha* consists of men and women committed to exploration and application of the teachings. During his lifetime many of these were homeless, living with few possessions in small communities. Today people take ordination as Buddhist monks and nuns, observing a wide range of precepts. These precepts do not allow the ordained person to kill animals, birds, fish or insects, bless troops or give support through any means whatsoever to any form of violent action in the world.

This tradition of the ordained *sangha* serves as a constant reminder to society that to resort to violence is the ultimate breakdown of communication. The Buddha has exhorted those who have realised the liberating significance of his teachings to "go forth for the welfare of all".

In our contemporary world, I believe this means we have to abandon the concept of the nation-state, so that there is a vision of life beyond self-interest, family interest, class interest and state interest. The underlying message which comes across from the Buddha is the necessity to act nonviolently and non-cooperatively in the face of violence, rather than be passive and indifferent.

On one occasion, the Buddha was told that two warring tribes were about to engage in a pitched battle. The Buddha walked to the location shortly before the battle was due to begin. He acted as a mediator. He bent down and picked up a piece of earth, and asked the two kings: "Is this bit of soil worth more than the blood of your friends and family?"

What is significant about the Buddha's teachings is that there is no endorsement of worship, religious rites, beliefs, ceremonies, or theistic or polytheistic interpretations of existence. The teachings offer a deeply religious life rendered meaningful through living with wisdom and mystery, with a deep and active reverence for people, creatures and environment - without belief in a God, saviour, holy book or prophet. Buddhism is thus safeguarded from religious wars, and from violence underpinned by intolerance arising from intense systems of belief, religious or national.

In the west today we are seeing a variety of movements with

a growing interest in these teachings. The peace movement, the green movement, the women's movement, the community of scientists, psychotherapists and social-political activists, are drawing on the wide range of practices, meditations, reflections and values embodied in the Buddhist tradition. The teachings offer the opportunity to discard what is not essential and to explore what is essential for freedom from suffering and injustice.

One thing that cannot be discarded in the teachings is the commitment to nonviolence.

The Buddhist Peace Fellowship UK can be contacted at 8 West Allington, Bridport, Dorset DT6 5BG.

Education

Tony Augarde

The basic principles of pacifism, because they are basic, are relevant in education as in most other fields. Among these principles we could include such things as the rejection of violence; the value of co-operation and reconciliation, as opposed to competition and conflict; the refusal to discriminate against people; and respect for the individual human personality.

These are only a few of the ideals of pacifism which have implications for the way we approach education. For example, our rejection of violence means that we shall reject such manifestations of violence as corporal punishment in schools. Our preference for co-operation over competition will lead us to question any division between pupil and pupil, or between teacher and pupil. If we refuse to discriminate against people on such grounds as race, colour or beliefs, we should also refuse to discriminate against them because of their level of intelligence or academic ability or home background. And our respect for the individuality of human beings saves us from seeing education as something to force people into a pre-determined pattern.

Education is a process whereby people can develop their personalities, their talents, their capacities. Education should bring out the best in people and help them to grow up aware, thoughtful, tolerant, happy and loving. Education is not restricted to places called schools or colleges, nor is it the prerogative of people called teachers. It is a process that continues through life, and it can be helped or hindered by schools and teachers.

Pacifists believe in the essential goodness of human beings, so we would advocate a child-centred education or person-centred education which seeks to help individuals to develop their own potential in the way best suited to them. This involves allowing opportunities for the emotions as well as the intellect to grow. Too many schools emphasise the head, and ignore the hands and the heart.

Children are born with a natural curiosity and are quickest to learn when they are interested in the subject. "Children, like adults, learn what they want to learn" (A S Neill). We wish to raise people, not sheep, and so we should encourage questioning and imagination. The most constructive use of children's energy is to allow them to learn, rather than trying to force them to learn something they are not interested in. Authoritarian adults often maintain that instruction, even indoctrination, is necessary because they know better than the child what is good for the child - but results usually prove them wrong. People only become self-disciplined by being allowed to discipline themselves, not by having discipline imposed upon them.

The authoritarian training in many schools accustoms children to depend upon other people for their standards and to 'do as they are told'. Such training leads to a blind acceptance of what our leaders tell us to do, and to a belief that we ourselves are powerless to solve human problems or change society. Hence the apathy and feeling of powerlessness among most people today, even in our 'democracy'.

In the present educational system, a fair degree of freedom is allowed children in many primary schools, although even here they are subjected to the 'hidden curriculum' which assumes that teachers know best and that there is always a right answer and a wrong answer. Less freedom is generally allowed in secondary schools, where authority is in the hands of the few: the head teacher and the staff, usually backed up by a fairly rigid hierarchy. The teachers have the 'right' answers, which the pupils are expected to accept, especially if they wish to succeed in exams.

Besides being trained not to question what authority hands out, pupils are generally discouraged from co-operating with one another. In fact they are encouraged to compete in almost everything - from exams to sport.

Competitiveness creates barriers between children, just as there are barriers between teachers and children. Our education system is characterised by many barriers: between those who are 'bright' and those who are 'dull'; between the academic and the practical; between one subject and another; between work and play; between school and the world outside.

Perhaps examinations constitute the greatest barrier in education today, since they not only obstruct co-operation between students but they are also responsible for much of the rigidity in syllabuses and the style of teaching. Tests of proficiency may be useful, but the stranglehold of exams is out of all proportion to any benefits they may convey. Examinations are by no means perfect tools: they are fallible and can test mainly short-term memory and subjects where there is a 'right' answer. By testing only what is examinable, exams encourage standardisation and devalue imagination; they lead to stagnant, irrelevant syllabuses and they divide knowledge into artificial boxes.

The subjects that are taught and examined in schools seldom have much relevance to real life. The range of what is taught is narrow - 'Science' usually only comprises Chemistry, Physics and Biology (omitting Psychology or Medicine); 'History' often concentrates on a narrow view of one's own country, excluding an understanding of the lives of ordinary people or a balanced view of the world. It is surely an indictment of schools that most of what is taught at them is forgotten by the pupils as soon as they have taken the exam, and the really important things are largely learnt outside schools.

Rigidity in the subjects that are taught is matched by rigidity in the way they are taught. Traditional methods are still observed - the teacher at the front of the class, giving information to pupils sitting at rows of desks. A semblance of order is maintained by artificial forms of discipline - rules and punishments - often backed by such relics of authoritarianism as school uniforms, prefects, and compulsory religious lessons or assemblies.

School itself should not be compulsory. Compulsory education may have served a purpose a hundred years ago, to save children from exploitation by industry, but today the main effect of compulsion is to create difficulties for teachers trying to cope with children who do not want to attend school. A change from compulsory to voluntary schooling would improve the atmosphere in education and would necessarily bring about changes in the way we consider and teach children.

The experience of progressive schools suggests that freedom does work, and that freedom, fulfilment and happiness are the most important qualities we should seek in education. Certainly most schools at present are failing to give children really valuable education - whether that be interpreted in the narrow utilitarian sense of something that fits them for life, or in the better, wider sense of something that allows them to develop in the best way possible and helps them to think for themselves.

A hundred years of compulsory education have not led us to a society free from war, violence, oppression, injustice, apathy, or any other of the evils that beset us. Indeed, the evidence suggests that our educational system is at least partly responsible for conditioning people to accept and perpetuate these evils. Everyone concerned for the future of society must be concerned to find better ways in education.

The Arts

Michael Tippett

A disciple, on one occasion, asks Confucius what he would consider the most important thing if he were entrusted with the government of a State, and he answers: *The rectification of the names* . . . For Confucius, names are not mere abstractions, but they signify something ideally co-ordinated with actuality. To each object, the name comes as the designation of its being. And if an object is correctly named, something essential is contained in the name regarding the nature of this object. While if an object is incorrectly named, then we tend to put the value we attach to the name onto the object, which will become thereby incorrectly valued. From this springs every sort of confusion.

Nothing is more desirable in our day than this rectification of the names, for in the deepening confusion we must constantly begin again at the beginning. To take an instance: there has been an attempt to prove that living beings are really only machines, and it has been shown that by habitually associating the sound of a bell with the eating of food, the mouths of dogs will water at the sound only. That physiological processes can be thus reduced to apparent mechanism is meant to convince us of the mechanical nature of life, which is thereby to receive the lower value of the machine, and the machine the higher value of life. Yet it would be hopeless to try and train a conditioned reflex by such means in a motor car, or even in a corpse. So that, in the end, 'life' and 'machine' are different names for different things. The rectification first enables us to speak of them correctly. To speak of them correctly will enable us to act correctly with regard to them - and so on.

Now, when value passes to the machine as against life, it also passes to Science as against Poetry. Everyone interested in this fundamental problem should read Willey: *Seventeenth Century Background*, which deals exhaustively with the artistic consequences of the division of sensibility into areas of 'true' statement (Science), and 'fiction' (Poetry). One of the significant trends of our time is that in films such as the Disney cartoons and the Marx Brothers, the mechanical 'facts' are being increasingly made to submit to the imaginative vision; that is, by arrangement and distortion, they are made into material for another class of experience than empirical observation. That value should be passing again to this other class of experience is a sign of the coming change in the climate of opinion.

The value, as a society, we put on art is not only affected by the division into 'fact' and 'fiction', but is also conditioned by our notions of morality. Thus the Greeks felt the concepts of the beautiful and the good to be so close together that they used the expression as one word. It took centuries of Christian teaching to break them apart and to arrive at a position where, with Puritanism, the beautiful is felt to be bad. But the Greek feeling seems to express something equally fundamental in us. Hence the strength of the humanist revival when it comes. "Exuberance is Beauty", said Blake.

The change of sensibility associated with such great names as Francis Bacon, Isaac Newton, Hobbes, Locke and Voltaire, led to the belief that human culture and progress were best obtained through technics. The result of this was that people came to feel the world of imagination as secondary and inferior. Art was reduced to decoration, and further debased to sentimentality. Either one said what one had to say in exact and virile prose, or one coated the pill with the sugar of poetry. Now, every material value which the technicians saw as springing from their discoveries was realised, and more. What they did not foresee was the paradox that the debasement of the world of imagination produced human beings incapable of using decently the material abundance thus produced. This has reached such dimensions that the material world is now destroying itself.

The outlook would be hopeless but for the fact that there is also now a conscious revolt against this condition. More and more people are born for whom the world of imagination is once more vital, if not decisive. Anyone who lives from the values of this inner world walks as a stranger through the world of technics.

The endless dualisms, of spirit-matter, imagination-fact, even down to that of class, have led to a position psychologically where modern humans are already born into division, and their capacity for balanced life is seriously weakened. Indeed, total war on its present scale is only possible because everyone is able in entire unconsciousness to project his inferior side on to the enemy. A lot of modern art attempts to find expression for the anguish of these divisions, but in the long run this state is fatal to art.

The only concept we can place over against the fact of the divided person is the idea of the whole person. If pacifists, for example, have to 'contract-out' of an intolerable social condition, they need to sense that they are 'contracting-in' to something more generous, rather as the early Christians 'contracted-out' of the Empire into a new abundance. Truly speaking, we are only able to contract-out of war into peace. The outward sign of such an inner health will be an abundance of creation, whether of values or works, in a world of destruction. This is why a pacifist-artist can be so positive.

The Media

Richard Keeble

The mass media are the dominant formulators of ideology in our society, the major sources of information about the contemporary world. Yet their control is in the hands of a tiny number of people.

Half the commercial television programmes, more than 66% of paperback and record sales, over 75% of women's magazine circulation, and more than 90% of national daily and Sunday paper circulation are controlled by the five leading companies in each sector. Many of the multinational corporations in control of newspaper groups also branch out into other media.

Along with this concentration of ownership has come a convergence of opinion within the media. On virtually every major issue, the national press speaks with one voice. For instance, during the late 1960s every national newspaper backed 'trade union reform'; all of them called for British entry into the Common Market during the referendum campaign in 1975; all of them backed James Callaghan for the leadership of the Labour Party and then later opposed Tony Benn's candidature for the deputy leadership. Fleet Street burst out into a chorus of jingoism over the Falklands crisis, and all on the Street of Shame profess to be "multilateralists".

Journalists, generally male, white and middle-class, largely internalise professional norms that attribute greater weight to sources from Establishment institutions rather than to the views of ordinary members of the public. They also largely share the assumptions and priorities of the dominant political culture. Thus the media, in reflecting the values of a materialistic, male-dominated, increasingly militaristic society, serve to legitimise and reinforce those values.

The media foster the belief that the political and social structure is natural, and they use the consensus as the framework for integrating and understanding events. Accordingly the Social Democratic Party, the consensus party *par excellence*, immediately won huge, sympathetic media coverage, while the peace movement is stigmatised as irrational and unrepresentative and confined to the political fringes.

Nowhere is the media's role of transmitting and thereby perpetuating the dominant values of capitalist society more clearly apparent than in its uncritical attitude towards militarism. The military metaphor is probably the most prevalent one in the media: their preoccupation with violence, shock, sensation and newness has its counterpart in the violence of their language and the violence of the stereotypes (racist, sexist, militaristic) which they perpetuate.

The media thrive on conflicts: inter-personal, social, political, economic. Trade unions make news when they go on strike. The vast amount of their other campaigning activities go generally unmentioned. News of Third World countries is largely confined to reports of warfare, poverty and natural disasters.

The militarisation of language and culture is particularly evident in the media's coverage of sport. For instance, the England team that beat Hungary in November 1981 were described by Stuart Jones in *The Times* as "Ron Greenwood's ageing soldiers". The home side won 1-0 but Jones described it thus: "England in the end had only one bullet in the barrel but it killed Hungary's meagre hopes". Sport, indeed, is always talked about in terms of attack, defence, victory, defeat, striking, shooting, battles, skirmishes, targets, onslaughts.

The special language of the nuclear age has been dubbed 'Nukespeak'. Just as in *1984* George Orwell described a centralist, repressive and militaristic state in which the rulers attempted to control language by creating the new language of "Newspeak"; so Paul Chilton analyses the way in which Nukespeak confirms and even directs people's attitudes and beliefs towards an acceptance of weapons of mass destruction.

A typical Nukespeak word is 'deterrent'. 'Deterrence' as a concept serves to legitimise the escalating arms race; it offers weaponry as a substitute for diplomatic or political resolution of differences. As E P Thompson says, the "deterrence theory freezes all political processes and increasingly, on both sides, constricts even cultural and intellectual exchanges within the same ideological parameters".

'Pacifist' also has its unique Nukespeak definition. According to this definition, it means idealist, utopian, unpatriotic, irrational, dangerously extremist left-wing. Reference to people as 'pacifist' immediately condemns them to the periphery of the political debate - exactly where politicians and their supporters in Fleet Street are struggling to confine the peace movement.

Other Nukespeak words, such as 'civil defence', 'demonstration bomb', 'clean weapons', 'limited nuclear war', are becoming alarmingly prevalent in the media.

E P Thompson has described the tame, multilateralist consensus over the nuclear arms issue as the 'doomsday consensus'. And, in his Bronowski Memorial Lecture, Dr Nicholas Humphrey commented on the way in which the media were preparing people for the holocaust. He described British society as being "full of fascinated spectators of the unfolding nuclear tragedy".

Equally people have for far too long been 'fascinated spectators' watching passively the rise of the mass media to their powerful positions of today. For their part, peace activists have for far too long indulged in nothing more than high-flown rhetoric of contempt of the media. And it is no longer enough simply to send off a letter of protest to an editor. There has to be action at all levels both against established media and towards the creation of new ones.

3. PACIFIST ACTION

What pacifists can do - and have done - to work for peace and against war, violence and injustice. The principles and practice of nonviolent action, and some examples of pacifist campaigns

Nonviolence

Howard Clark

"Neither victim nor executioner" - to Albert Camus' phrase I would add "but nonviolent activist". For nonviolence is fundamentally the search for alternatives to practising violence or submitting to injustice and oppression.

Nonviolent actions begin with recognition of the violence inherent in the status quo, in social relationships of domination. Its first action may often be refusal - both refusal to violate, perhaps merely by cooperating with the violence that upholds a system of domination, and refusal to be a victim. But behind this refusal is a commitment and a vision: a commitment to give people more control of their own lives and a vision of a social order where human beings can fulfil their potential for good.

A few nonviolent actions are heroic: none more so than the defiance of soldiers in tanks by unarmed people in Beijing and Manila in the 1980s and Prague in 1968. Many nonviolent actions are dramatic, seeking to demonstrate the illegitimacy of a regime - for instance, South African Blacks seeking to bathe on a Whites-only beach; or to alert the world to crimes against humanity - for instance, people entering nuclear testing zones. Some involve thousands of people and aim to instill a sense of their own power for change - demonstrations, strikes, boycotts. Some happen on the quiet, for instance when shipbuilders in

Nazi-occupied Denmark contrived to 'misunderstand' orders and do their work so badly that the ship they were building could not be used in the war.

In extremes, a pacifist would rather die than kill - the same attitude shown by many of the students in Tiananmen Square. The primary focus, however, is not on the extreme but on the many smaller choices to be made, the points where people act out of habitual obedience or construct their vision to the 'normal' political routines. The constant endeavour of nonviolence is therefore to emphasise that we do have choices and to suggest that there are alternatives.

In most movements of mass unarmed struggle, there are likely to be relatively few complete pacifists. But movements which adopt nonviolence because in their particular situation it offers the most effective way of challenging entrenched power, implicitly acknowledge some of the key points of nonviolence. Their success depends on their appreciation of the dynamics of nonviolent action and insights which are an essential part of the philosophy of nonviolence.

You don't have to believe in nonviolence in principle to welcome methods of social change which do not depend on equipping and training yourselves with the weapons of war and building up military command structures, but which are open to all the community. You don't have to be a pacifist to acknowledge the strategic power of nonviolence in a social struggle: its ability to empower the hopeless and powerless; its impact in creating dilemmas for the oppressor and its capacity to provoke divisions within a ruling elite. A realist can see the wisdom of the non-violent insistence that today's antagonist may be tomorrow's neighbour; on distinguishing between a person and the oppressive role they are currently playing; and above all that the means pursued in a social struggle will condition the future.

Oppressive power structures ultimately depend on the acquiescence of the majority of the people: the power of the people often rests in withdrawing consent from the system of government, both by non-cooperation and through setting up autonomous parallel structures. Most discussion on nonviolent action tends to concentrate on methods of resistance and non-cooperation. For Gandhi, however, the centre of nonviolent strategy lay in its programme for social reconstruction. The priority was to try to build a new society beginning at the base by

97

behaving differently in everyday life. Independence would not begin only after the British had left; it had to be a process beginning now with internal reform, the colonised society regaining its fitness for self-government.

Originally, Gandhi's constructive programme began by stressing three points: most famously, the spinning wheel and the wearing of homespun cloth, but also, less symbolically, sanitation and literacy. As the movement progressed, the constructive programme expanded to address other points - for instance, overcoming 'untouchability' in the caste system and seeking the uplift of women - until by the end of his life Gandhi saw it as the daily embodiment of a nonviolent value system. It was also a form of training in nonviolence and a way of involving people in the movement for social change without necessarily engaging them in direct confrontation with authority. Small steps which began in people's daily lives grew into larger organisations - such as cooperatives for the distribution of homespun cloth, centres for basic education, and programmes for land redistribution. By the end of his life, Gandhi saw nonviolence largely in terms of constructive programme. Methods of direct resistance and confrontation would come into play when the powers-that-be obstructed the growth of the new society.

For its contemporary adherents, nonviolence remains something that has to be rooted in everyday life. This has many aspects: from the conduct of our interpersonal relationships to an awareness of the impact of our lifestyle on people in other countries and on the planet itself. The systems which threaten the world - militarily, ecologically, economically - seem out of human control. The nonviolent response is not to look for technological fixes but to identify where and how we can affect these systems, to pose fundamental moral and social questions directed not only at the ruling elites - the people most responsible - but also at ourselves and behaviour in our everyday lives. What can *we* do?

As in large-scale social struggle, in everyday life nonviolence does not seek to deny conflict but to bring about creative resolutions: encouraging people to stand up for themselves, challenging patterns of domination and submission, finding non-destructive ways of expressing anger, and witnessing to a larger vision and certain fundamental principles. Nonviolence seeks to create a culture that values the basic humanity of all people, that looks not for dominion over the earth but harmony with it, that cherishes diversity but also celebrates what people have in common, and that both practises and defends basic freedom and rights.

Nonviolence is visionary in seeking new possibilities, but also responsible in recognising the costs of a struggle and in recognising limits. One of the reasons human survival is now at peril is the widespread failure to recognise limits, but probably for the adherent of nonviolence the limits most difficult to accept are those on what we can achieve.

Our philosophy calls for revolutionary social changes yet, at times, only smaller changes seem to be on the social agenda. Movements are repressed or become isolated. Social attitudes move against the values we want to promote. Vaclav Havel, the Czech playwright (who was rapidly transformed by popular nonviolent action from political prisoner to president), has written of the necessity to "live in the truth". Even when hopes are dim, this is the kernel of nonviolence. We cannot predict the fruits of our behaviour but we can be sure that life would not be worth living if the values of nonviolence were extinguished.

Conscientious Objection

Peace Pledge Union members

'Conscientious objection' is a term applied to an individual objection, on grounds of conscience, to being conscripted for military service. For some people this leads to the acceptance of alternative service. For others, often called 'absolutists' or 'total resisters', no form of directed service is acceptable.

Conscription for full-time military service was first introduced in Britain in 1916. The Military Service Act which made this compulsory included a clause that legalised the right to claim exemption on grounds of conscience. This clause was inserted only after arduous campaigning by pacifists in the No-Conscription Fellowship. However, the 'conscience clause' was poorly administered, with a military representative playing a prejudicial part in the tribunals set up to hear applications for registration as conscientious objectors (COs).

The result was that many conscientious objectors in World War I were harshly treated. A few who resolutely refused to have any part in the war were sentenced to death by the military courts and, though their sentences were eventually commuted to ten years' imprisonment, they endured the torment of being taken to France, ostensibly to be shot. Many others were given prison sentences of up to two years, with repeated sentences when they continued to refuse. Out of some 16,000 COs, 73 died as a result of the conditions they had to put up with. In those days, too, conscientious objection was so little understood by the majority of people that those who refused conscription were often the victims of ostracism and scorn.

In World War II, when not only men but some women were conscripted, the responsibility for dealing with COs was more clearly a civilian matter and on the whole more humanely administered; although there were still instances of conscientious objectors being sent to prison because tribunals refused recognition. The majority of the 60,000 COs were, however, granted exemption from military service conditional upon their agreeing to perform some alternative service: in a hospital, on the land or in social service, for example. In both wars, a very few were granted total exemption.

British conscription ended in 1960. Nowadays, members of the armed forces can claim discharge on the grounds of having become conscientious objectors after joining. These COs are often helped by pacifists in organisations such as *At Ease*, which offers advice and assistance to those who wish to leave the forces on conscientious grounds.

In contrast to Britain, where conscription has applied only from 1916 to 1919 and from 1939 to 1960, most countries in Europe have had compulsory military service since the 19th century. Most European countries made no provision for conscientious objection during the Second World War, though Denmark operated an alternative-service law even during German occupation; the Netherlands had some provision, and Sweden too. Until 1939 the USSR also had some provision, but this appears to have lapsed with the introduction of the Universal Service Law of that year.

It was not until well after 1945 that the right of conscientious objection became more widely accepted, and that was only because people like Louis Lecoin in France, Pietro Pinna in Italy, Jean van Lierde in Belgium, Pepe Beunza in Spain and Michaelis Laraggakis in Greece went on hunger-strike and suffered imprisonment until public opinion was stirred.

Only in 1987 did the UN Commission on Human Rights recognise conscientious objection as a basic and universal human right, but that is hedged by the 'right' of states to impose other obligatory service - often significantly longer than the normal military period - and to make some 'test' of conscience. Even the European Parliament admitted in 1983 that 'no court or commission can penetrate the conscience of an individual'.

Despite all this, conscription without proper provision for COs continues in NATO countries like Turkey, neutral Switzerland, military-dominated countries in Latin America, and the 'people's republic' of China. In eastern Europe, conscientious objection is at last being gradually accepted, and there is even official discussion in the Soviet Union of abolishing conscription altogether. Meanwhile in Israel women are conscripted without rights of conscience, and in South Africa only Whites are conscripted or, like David Bruce, face up to six years in prison.

The growing resistance to conscription is not an individual but a social phenomenon. It is not merely a question of trying to avoid the persecution of a few individuals with unorthodox religious views or unusually tender consciences. Conscientious objectors are making a stand not for themselves alone but for a principle of universal importance. Non-conformists are always a nuisance to governments, but it is due to the non-conformists of the past that we have many of the liberties we enjoy today.

Northern Ireland: Doing Something Constructive

Will Warren

This account of my six years in Derry tells of some of the experiences of an ordinary person in the midst of struggle.

If there was one thing I learned in Northern Ireland, it was the futility of violence. On several occasions, I was the bearer of threats of one sort or another. It was at such times that I was able to express a point of view that offered another course of action. That I was sometimes successful is an indication that the paramilitaries are honest when they declare that they only adopt violence as a last resort. The tragedy is that all too often no other avenue is offered to them. Once people think of them as 'terrorists' and cut off communication, the gunmen lose touch with ordinary people, and in so doing narrow down their choice of action. I'm certain that it was only because I treated them as friends that I had any influence at all. They also had an influence on me to the extent that they treated me as a friend. That is how reconciliation works. It is not a one-way flow but a penetrating interchange of ideas, often leading to new solutions.

Children took up a deal of my time. When I first squatted in a house in the strongly Republican area of the Brandywell, small children watched me move in. Some of them helped me. After that, they came in whenever they wanted, often straight from school, staying until I turned them out when I wanted to go to bed. Frequently they cooked meals for me. Many times they were engaged in running fights with the British army and rushed into the house when attacked with CS gas. On one occasion, I packed 17 of them into my mini (designed to hold four) and drove them over the border, a couple of miles away, so that they could get some fresh air. This delighted them and gave rise to a custom whereby I took car loads of them out when I could. The parents got to know me, and the paramilitaries decided I was not too bad if I cared for their children.

After the Provos had created their 'no go' areas, they found it necessary to form their own police force, called 'Vigilantes'. When I had been living in the area some months, I was invited to join. I accepted. Although most of their function was really to police the district and was performed with no violence, whenever it appeared that the British army was about to enter they ceased to be vigilantes and became paramilitaries. This provided an opportunity for me. I invariably moved away from my comrades toward the army and stood in the middle of the road, to the surprise and consternation of my friends, who were fearful for my safety. It then became easy, indeed inevitable, for me to explain my philosophy of nonviolence. As I had demonstrated my concern for the well-being of the community at large and their children, and also my willingness to share the work of policing, they accepted my sincerity and acknowledged the fact that nonviolence does not mean simply opting out of the struggle. It does not mean standing on the sidelines watching others do the work and face the danger. The fact that I was English helped, for it was not my struggle but theirs I was concerned with.

Some students hired a coach to take children out for the day, inviting 25 Catholics. They then decided to take Protestants as well, but they knew none. I was asked to find some for them. This I thought would be easy. I approached the Democratic Unionist Party, and the local organiser willingly agreed to the proposal. The day arrived, but no Protestants. The next day, I found out why the children had not turned up: ''We could only get 24 and it was not advisable to go as a minority: our children would have been beaten up''.

On another occasion, I had a number of Catholic children in my van and decided to invite some Protestants. The children beseeched me not to, as they might be outnumbered. So I took one Catholic boy to the Waterside and slowed down outside the house of a friend. As I expected, a lot of boys and girls rushed out begging for a ride. I invited them in. After a long period of silence, I told Johnnie, the Catholic boy, to change seats so a Protestant child could sit in front. He moved back among the Protestant children and more silence ensued. But eventually I heard ''What's your name?'' ''Johnnie''. A pause, then ''What's yours?'' ''Dean''. By the time we had finished the run, they were chattering away like normal children. Later, I was able to return with a number of Catholics, who were apprehensive, but reassured by John.

So I broke down the fear in the hearts of a few children. A small, token act. But it was worthwhile. Reconciliation is always slow. But, once effected, it is - I believe - lasting.

At one time there were riots in a particular road, commencing at ten minutes past three. The schools finish at three and it takes ten minutes to walk to the army post on William Street, which children were determined to destroy. In the end they succeeded, beginning with cat-calls followed by stone-throwing and, eventually, arson. I didn't see anyone over school age engaged in this. Flushed with success, the children proceeded to burn down the little houses, some occupied by old people, in a side street. Next, they were ready to start on William Street. The army was determined to prevent them; so the children got reinforcements in the shape of their elders, and confrontation followed.

Having moved into the side street about this time, I decided I should walk through the riots. For some three months, I did this nearly every day. At first stones, rubber bullets and gas canisters were thick in the air, many narrowly missing me. Sometimes the soldiers apologised for nearly hitting me. As the days passed, I noticed the stone throwing slow down until finally, as I quietly walked down the street, the soldiers held their fire and the rioters likewise.

It is difficult to assess the result of this kind of action (as in so many things I did), or to explain exactly why I did these things, apart from an inner sense of rightness. Primarily, I wanted to demonstrate that there is something more powerful than what comes out of the barrel of a gun. Also I wanted to show that I was neither pro-army or pro-rioter, but pro-people.

One evening I was asked to go along to the Apprentice Boys' Hall, where there was a phone call from Belfast for me. It was the Ulster Defence Association leadership calling to say that two of their members had been murdered, it was thought by Derry Provos. The UDA proposed to murder six Derry Catholics that night in reprisal, unless I could assure them within an hour that no Derry person was involved. An hour wasn't enough time, I protested; I must have at least two. They agreed. I hurried around to the Bogside, where I was lucky to find the man I wanted; he assured me that no one in Derry knew anything of the murders. I rushed back home and telephoned Belfast just in time to prevent a party of men from setting out for Derry. It is interesting that each side accepted the word of the other, something I found to be true on numerous occasions. All that was necessary was to have a trusted intermediary.

I went to Derry with no preconceived plan of action. While I was there, I tried to work out my concern day by day as seemed best. Had I had a different upbringing, I might very well have behaved in a different way, but everyone must behave in the way that seems right at the time. What really matters is that each of us tries to do what we can.

Norwegian Pacificism under the Occupation

Diderich H Lund

During the Second World War, as in most occupied countries, a strong resistance movement grew up in Norway. Unlike them, however, was its nonviolent nature. It is true that there was also a secret military organisation, the Milorg, partly consisting of soldiers trained in Britain and brought secretly into Norway. But it was the unarmed resistance of the civilians that sustained the nation and kept it united during the occupation.

After the resistance became organised, an underground press was established to publish the facts and counteract the bewildering propaganda, and to print for distribution among the people 'paroles' advising them when to obey and when to refuse a German order. The 'paroles' were valuable in giving a feeling to the population that in some way justice and order still reigned, and as a rule they were obeyed by practically everyone concerned. The Germans could do nothing but accept the situation and, in spite of their strenuous efforts to wipe out the secret presses, and the many thousands of Norwegians who lost their lives or were imprisoned and tortured, nothing could silence the voice of the press. New helpers were ready at any moment to fill the empty places, and new printing presses were always available.

Perhaps the most dangerous underground activity was the propaganda among the German troops. Not much of this work was done by the Norwegians, but we saw instances of excellent and daring propaganda by the German soldiers themselves, done at tremendous risk.

Service in and around the concentration camps set up by the Germans opened a new field of activity to daring youth. Contact had to be made between prisoners and the outside world, to tell prisoners which of their comrades, safely out of reach, they could name to the Gestapo if torture became unbearable, or to find out which had been named and were in danger. Now and then, a prisoner threatened with torture and death had to be taken out of prison by some stratagem.

Hiding places were arranged for those hunted by the Gestapo. The homes of elderly ladies were much preferred for this, and many of them sheltered fugitives constantly throughout the war years. But the solidarity was so general and widespread that one had the feeling one might enter any door and ask for protection. It was necessary also to give financial support to those who had lost their income as a result of engaging in resistance work, or those left behind by people who had escaped or who had been imprisoned or executed; but everyone contributed, and it was never difficult to get the money.

Although the nonviolent resistance movement did not make use of sabotage in its military form as did the Milorg, sabotage in factories or in administration that impeded German activities was accepted. These activities, however, including occasionally the necessary destruction of the Germans' records and documents by fire or explosion, were carried out without violence to the Germans - only Norwegian lives were at stake.

But *secret* warfare is not always the most advisable. One of the most inspiring features of the unarmed resistance in Norway was its open and uncompromising nature, expressed from the first moment by so many, and by individuals as well as groups, at the risk of liberty and of life.

The first resistance came, perhaps somewhat unexpectedly, from the hundreds of thousands of youths in the athletic clubs. The Nazis tried to take over control of the clubs, probably to use them eventually for military ends. Immediately all organised athletic activity ceased, and remained in abeyance for the five years of the occupation.

The next to resist was the Supreme Court of Justice, whose members resigned their offices when the Germans tried to reshape the fundamental principles of justice in the image of the Nazi system.

But the people who most of all became the prototypes of our spiritual resistance and unarmed struggle were our teachers and clergy. All along the line, the teachers refused to follow Nazi orders to alter their teaching to accord with Nazi principles, and the teachers took the consequences of their resistance. Hundreds were sent to prison or to compulsory labour in the Arctic; schools were closed, though to some extent teaching went on secretly in the homes of the pupils. After six months privation and suffering in the frigid climate of Finnmark, the teachers won, and the Germans sent them home and allowed them to resume their work.

Just as important was the undaunted and unflinching resistance of the Church. It was directed, with fine discrimination, not against the occupying power as such, but against the anti-Christian measures of the occupying power, and it tried to keep away from the nationalistic resistance.

The clergymen and the bishops resigned their offices as civil servants, and the salaries attached to them. But they went on with their work as preachers and the spiritual leaders of their parishioners, until they were forcibly transferred to places where the Germans hoped that they would be harmless. The leaders were sent to prison or to concentration camps; but the seed they had sown bore fruit many times over and, in one way or another, most of those who were left continued their activity. The dissenting churches joined the State Church in its resistance with the same courage and ability.

Many more instances of open resistance could be enumerated, such as the open letter signed with the names and addresses of several hundred thousand parents protesting against the Nazis' efforts to win the children to their creed. These open demonstrations were the essence of the unarmed resistance: they made it a struggle of the whole people, a struggle in which everyone felt they were playing an important part, and in which there was a place for young and old, for women and men.

War Tax Resistance

William   Hetherington

Few people enjoy paying taxes, but most of us accept that there must be some means of sharing amongst the community the cost of public services. We may each have our reservations about particular forms and levels of taxation but the principle is generally accepted. Why should pacifists or other peace campaigners make special objection?

It needs to be remembered that war has had a particular effect on taxation. Income tax, for example, was specifically invented by William Pitt in 1799 to raise funds for the French Revolutionary War. Although it was originally conceived as a temporary measure, all attempts permanently to abolish it failed in the face of continuing conflicts up to the Crimean War. Since that time it has made a fundamental contribution to Government revenue, out of which funding borrowings for past wars and the planning of future wars is an ever-increasing charge.

The direct connection between taxation and spending on war is not difficult to see, and the idea of resisting war in this way is by no means new. Henry Thoreau wrote of mid-nineteenth century Massachusetts: "If a thousand men were not to pay their tax bills this year, that would not be a violent and bloody measure, as it would be to pay them, and enable the State to commit violence and shed innocent blood. This is, in fact, the definition of a peaceable revolution if any such is possible".

It was an aspect of the 'Never again' mood of 1930s Britain that a number of people risked imprisonment rather than pay that part of their income tax which was attributable to war preparation. PAYE - the Pay As You Earn system - introduced in 1940 as a relatively painless method of enforcing payment for the Second World War, has made tax resistance virtually impossible for many citizens to implement but has by no means reduced interest in it as a political method. Indeed, in the 1960s and again in the

1980s there has been a resurgence of war tax resistance, which has reflected the increasing concern of people to prepare for peace in the face of continued planning for war.

There was a time when military expenditure was mainly the pittance paid to soldiers, basic subsistence and elementary weapons. Manpower (there were thankfully no women soldiers) counted rather than money. One of the factors of modern warfare is that a far higher proportion of material resources in relation to personpower is required. Sophisticated technological weaponry needs few people to operate it but is extremely expensive to produce and maintain, as is the training of the personnel involved. This is the main reason why the military authorities are not interested in conscription as a form of recruitment, they need quality rather than quantity of personnel.

This means both that the occasion for pacifists to refuse military service (a principle recognised in British law since 1916) no longer normally arises and that the significance of the financial contribution of us all is much greater than formerly. On figures provided by the Government, each income-taxpayer contributes on average more than £2 *every day* of the year to 'Defence'. The question therefore arises as to whether we should refuse the conscription of our usually hard-earned money in the same way that previously many of us would refuse conscription of our bodies.

Pacifists have therefore proposed two complementary resolutions of this dilemma. As a result of an initiative within the Peace Pledge Union in 1977, the Peace Tax Campaign, now a peace organisation in its own right, came into being. The object of this campaign is to bring about legislation enabling taxpayers to indicate that the portion of their taxes which would normally be spent on war and war preparation - euphemistically termed 'defence' - should be diverted to some precisely designated peaceful purpose. Clearly many details would need to be worked out, but the principle is seen as analogous to the concept of legally recognised alternative civilian service during the time of military conscription.

That is necessarily a long-term objective, and therefore gives rise to the other more immediate method of enabling conscientious objection to military taxes. Just as in countries where there is no legal provision for conscientious objection to military service, some objectors simply refuse to serve regardless of what the law says; so some people refuse to pay the military proportion of their taxes, regardless of the present rigours of the law. The withheld tax is usually placed in a special account, to make clear that it is readily available for peace preparation, but not war preparation.

It is sometimes argued that there is an overriding duty to obey every law, at least of a democratic society. That, however, is nothing less than an abdication of one's conscience to the government, which is the seed of totalitarianism. Most people refrain from murder not because there is a law against it but because conscience forbids it. In matters of ethics the reverse principle also applies: in the same way that the Nuremburg judgement placed the dictates of common humanity before the outward forms of law, so we all have a duty to question any authority, however exalted. It may well be that in most matters we are prepared to accept the decision of others or make some compromise. On issues of deep principle, however, we have to take a stand or cease to be true to ourselves. For pacifists, war and war preparation is such an issue. If one conscientiously objects to taking part in war, then conscientiously objecting to paying for war is the clear corollary. No-one has the right to kill. No-one has the right to order another to kill. No-one has the right to order another to pay for the means of killing.

A considerable number of people, not only in Britain but also abroad, have resisted payment of war taxes in this way. For some, this has resulted in imprisonment, and others have had their personal possessions seized and sold. Because of the PAYE system, the great majority in Britain have been self-employed people, but the Society of Friends (the Quakers) as an employer has attempted to make provision for the consciences of its employees. The Peace Pledge Union decided in 1982 that as a pacifist organisation it ought not to be the channel for the collection of war taxes, and therefore as an employer has refused to pass on the military proportion of PAYE deductions. The PPU has also refused to pay the war-tax proportion due on its own taxable income. After six and a half years the Inland Revenue obtained a court order to remove an amount for the first four years' tax from the PPU's account, but that still left the PPU as the longest-running case of war-tax resistance in British history as resistance continues.

Militarism takes many expensive forms in our society. Withdrawing our cash is the most telling means of withdrawing our consent to the activities and attitudes which lead to the hopeless destructiveness of war. In its place pacifists are concerned to devote financial resources, as they would human and natural resources, to curing and caring, healing and helping. Peace itself cannot be brought in simple money terms, but by refusing to pay for war we can encourage the growth of the things that make for peace.

Remembrance

Lucy Beck

> But the past is just the same - and War's a bloody game . . .
> Have you forgotten yet? . . .
> Look down, and swear by the slain of the War that
> you'll never forget.

Siegfried Sassoon's moving anti-war poetry challenges us to
remember the millions who died on the battlefields of the First
World War. Each year the State and the British Legion organise
official Remembrance ceremonies and red poppies are sold to
help the military victims of the world wars. But the Peace Pledge
Union does not believe this is what Sassoon meant by 'never
forget'. To meet each year for a brief ceremony, heavily over-
laid by the trappings and nostalgia of war, is not to learn the
lessons of those tragic conflicts. Millions are still dying in wars all
over the world.

The Peace Pledge Union has taken up the challenge to
remember all those who died and are dying in war, by working to
prevent wars ever happening again. Remembrance has come to
the forefront of the PPU's work as it symbolises everything the
PPU stands for. The PPU's pledge is drawn from an Armistice
Day sermon, and it was Dick Sheppard who first challenged the
nature of the official Remembrance ceremonies in 1925. His own
experiences in the First World War led him to found the PPU, as
they led Sassoon to become a PPU sponsor. It was women bereft
of husbands and sons in that war who chose the white poppy
symbol for the Women's Co-operative Guild in 1933 as 'a pledge
to peace that war must not happen again'. Both groups promoted
the white poppy in the late 1930s, organised alternative ceremonies to lay white poppy wreaths, and encouraged the holding of
Peace Days and Weeks at Remembrance time.

The mass distribution and sale of white poppies was revived

in the 1980s, and the PPU also organises alternative Remembrance ceremonies each year at the Cenotaph and a silent vigil outside the British Legion's Festival of Remembrance. Other white poppy wreaths are laid by local groups at their war memorials. The PPU's white poppy wreath bears the inscription 'When Shall We Ever Learn?', calling for remembrance of all those dying in wars today and of the forgotten victims such as civilians and refugees, and drawing attention to the British involvement in those wars through the arms trade.

The PPU's challenge to what has become a national institution led in 1986 to a question to the Prime Minister in the House of Commons. Her condemnation of white poppies stimulated lively debate throughout the country in local and national press and media which still continues. It has drawn attention publicly to fundamental questions about war and its validity as a means of solving conflict. Each year more and more people are joining with the PPU by wearing the white poppy of peace at Remembrance time and pledging themselves to work for peace throughout the year.

Children and War

Jan Melichar

War begins in our minds and so, if we want peace, it is in our minds that it will have to be constructed. The way that we bring up the young - the values that we introduce them to - will have a powerful effect on the shape and nature of society in the future.

These are two fairly simple propositions with which most people will be able to agree in general terms. However, the moment one starts to tease out some of the implications of such views, everything falls apart.

The Peace Pledge Union began the Children and War Project to put some coherence and order into the mass of apparently conflicting arguments, to focus on some of the key issues, and to uncover some of the hidden meanings behind the rhetoric of war and peace. It aims to put these issues much higher on the public agenda and encourage a more rational debate about the causes of war.

Whilst the Project focuses on children, it is aimed at adults who are the transmitters of values and beliefs to the young. It thus challenges us all to scrutinise our own values more carefully and start to understand how these have been shaped. An examination of this shaping process is seen as vital not only to our understanding why the willingness to kill strangers permeates most of modern society but more importantly to help us recognise that we not only have a choice but also the power to re-shape the landscape of the future.

Without change, today's children will become the next generation that continues the same processes of war preparation and war making. It is a process that has its roots in an 'invisible values system' which is 'taught' to a child from the moment of birth and is reinforced by social practices and institutions. From the hierarchical relationship within a family, through the distancing of peoples from each other in family units, through an educational system which has embedded within it competitiveness as a prime value, to the adult world where we compete against each other for survival, an antagonistic system has been created and has come to appear natural. 'Natural' used in this way implies that, whatever it is, it cannot be changed. But 'natural' ought not to remain the modern-day version of original sin which disempowers us and strips us of the burden of responsibility.

As this is too vast an area for the Project to explore, it takes as a symbol the 'war toy', not so much the war toy as an object but the values embedded within it. In the same way that fighting wars and preparing for them seems 'natural' and right, so too is playing with war toys seen as natural and harmless. Both beliefs have similar origins, and neither is 'true'.

A peaceful future requires that we no longer promote beliefs and values, attitudes and experience, which glorify and enhance war and violence in the child's mind. We must, therefore, confront those institutions and practices in society which foster such views, while we at the same time promote humane and co-operative values.

4. ALTERNATIVES

What alternatives can pacifists suggest,
as ways of moving towards a more
peaceful society?

Peace Education

James McCarthy

There are two kinds of objection to the study of peace in schools: first, that its content is dangerous (because it may lead to appeasement or indoctrination in some form); second, that any discussion of political issues within schools is not 'education' and should therefore be avoided.

Keeping politics out of education is not only extremely difficult in practice: who decides what is 'political', what criteria do they use, and how are their decisions given effect? It is also highly questionable in theory, since it is precisely the attempt to keep controversial issues out of the curriculum that is likely to lead to charges of indoctrination. Where no awkward questions are asked, there is the beginning of the end of freedom.

The other charge, that the study of peace could lead to attitudes conducive to appeasement, is based on two kinds of confusion. First is the assumption that there is no viable method of resisting aggression other than by armed force. This is a popular view but it is open to question, particularly in the light of the many examples of nonviolent resistance and nonviolent change around the world: examples which might form part of a course in peace studies.

Second is the assumption that peace education involves a simple transfer of attitude from teacher to pupil. But peace education is a complex subject in which questions of attitude need to be separated from, as well as integrated with, questions of fact and value. The elucidation of facts alone must be a major part of any study of war and peace. The dimensions of the arms race, its direction and effects, deserve detailed study; not only because this is the basis from which any talk of peace must begin but also because the interpretation of the facts themselves demands careful scrutiny.

Perhaps one of the most important values of peace studies is as a defence against indoctrination. Yet peace education itself is often equated with indoctrination. This is to forget that the education system is not neutral but purveys a host of clearly defined attitudes which are relayed to it by the wider society and are embedded in its structure. This 'hidden curriculum' is the more powerful because it is hidden. It includes a pervasive emphasis on hierarchy, grading and competition; acceptance of the necessity of regulating behaviour by a system of reward and punishment; the assumption that examinations are the *point* of education and that performing well in them is a result of intelligence and will lead to a better job and higher status in the world outside.

Fundamentally, many school processes are dictated by assumptions and forces which are beyond the pupils' power to question or influence; these processes are thus unlikely to reflect the pupils' own needs and wishes. Peace studies must at some point question these assumptions, since a just society is unlikely to emerge from an education system of this kind.

Militarism, too, finds its way into the hidden curriculum. The army recruiting advertisements impinge to some extent on the consciousness of most schoolboys and girls. The excitement and glamour of firing real guns are made available to some, via cadet forces, with the full co-operation of the school. Co-operation of this kind is vital in securing a continuing public acceptance of official militarism in years to come.

If, on the other hand, the role of the armed forces is a subject for enquiry and discussion in school, in a peace studies course or elsewhere, if the implications of militarism along with other aspects of the hidden curriculum are open to discussion and modification, then a new awareness may begin to open - and it is awareness that leads to free and responsible choice.

Peace education, in the end, is about the making of such choices. It should have as its aim the emergence of unfettered minds, of people unafraid of new ideas and experiences, able to make independent judgements about themselves and their place in society. The worst way to achieve this result would be to preach pacifism - or anything else. What is the best way is a matter for enquiry, debate and thorough adventurous experimentation.

Education for Peace, edited by David Hicks in 1988, listed the following likely trends for peace education in the 1990s:

1. *World studies* There will be an increasing interest in world studies programmes, and projects such as *World Studies 8-13*, as providing a practical and clear embodiment of education for peace principles in action.

2. *Anti-racism* There will be increasing recognition that peace education must be anti-racist in its stance, and a realisation that anti-racism can learn from the insights of peace education.

3. *Gender* Peace education practitioners will play their part in developing anti-sexist curricula and equal opportunities for girls and women, and in challenging male socialisation into patterns of violence.

4. *Human rights* There will be increasing emphasis on teaching and learning about justice, rights and responsibilities, in local, national and international contexts.

5. *Media* Increasing attention will be paid to the role of the media in influencing children's attitudes towards violence as well as affecting the formation of their views of the world.

6. *World development* There will be a continued emphasis on teaching about North-South issues, and increasing links with those involved in development education and with Development Education Centres.

7. *Controversy* More consideration will be given to clarifying the characteristics of indoctrination and to the specific professional and ethical responsibilities of teachers when teaching about controversial issues.

8. *International links* There will be increasing links with peace and global education initiatives, especially with Europe, the USA, Australia and Canada.

9. *National curriculum* Careful attention will be given to the ways in which specific subject areas can contribute to an understanding of issues to do with peace and conflict as well as to the ways in which they can benefit from peace education methodology.

10. *Process* The process of person-centred education and active learning will be continually reaffirmed, and particular attention will be given in this respect to classroom management and school organisation.

Peace Studies

Adam Curle

Having spent many years concerned with Third World problems and being much moved by the violence and suffering I saw, I attempted to understand its origins. Then, over a period of four or five years, I was directly involved in mediation efforts in wars in Africa and Asia, and my rudimentary ideas on peace and violence began to focus on problems of international negotiation. However, even as I developed my conclusions, I realised that my approach was too narrow. A skilful negotiator might ease a particular situation, but the circumstances, the rivalries, the oppression, the scarcity of resources - which had given rise to it - remained. Moreover, even if wars are brought to an end, many of the conditions associated with war continue throughout large areas of the world. People are driven from their homes, unjustly imprisoned, separated from their families, flung into detention camps, virtually enslaved, exploited by landlords, victimised by the police, oppressed by the government, starved and malnourished because of official neglect and official policies. They are humiliated and have their perceptions distorted by propaganda; many in fact die because of these conditions. Circumstances such as these inflict such damage on human life, health, capacity for creative and happy existence and work, and for the development of potential, that I find it impossible to refer to them as peaceful. They inflict upon human beings, though in a less concentrated form, many of the same destructive horrors as does war.

From my perception of these circumstances I drew three conclusions. Firstly, the study of peace should not be confined to the analysis of means of preventing or terminating wars. Secondly, because many of these circumstances are intra- rather than international, the study of peace should not be considered as exclusively on the international level. Thirdly, support for a *status quo* which permitted or encouraged such unpeaceful conditions could in no sense be considered as the promotion of peace: on the contrary, it was the tacit condoning of violence.

The concept of peace I found, however, to be unsatisfactory. It was too vague, too emotive and too manipulable. I therefore developed an approach based on what I termed peaceful and unpeaceful relations - between individuals, groups or nations. I defined peaceful relationships as those in which individuals or groups can achieve together goals which they could not have reached separately; or at least do not impede each other. Unpeaceful relationships are those in which the units concerned damage each other so that in fact they achieve less than they could have done independently; and in one way or another harm each other's capacity for growth, maturation or fulfilment. Or they are relationships in which one party suffers in this fashion, even if the other does not and may indeed appear to gain the advantage, as a conqueror might gain advantage through conquest.

The first task of Peace Studies is to identify and analyse these relationships. The next function is to use this information in order to devise means of changing unpeaceful into peaceful relationships. Here theory and practice may become closely related. There must be concern for changing perceptions, for enlarging awareness of social reality: and there must be concern for changing the balance of power where strength is being employed to enhance or maintain the strong at the expense of the weak.

Thus, certain unpeaceful relations can only move towards a peaceful character after a period of change, even turmoil, in which, paradoxically, Peace Studies must be implicated: seeking nonviolent approaches towards changing the *status quo*, for it would seem to me inconsistent to repay one sort of violence with another. It is also clearly a task for Peace Studies to examine the process of negotiation very carefully, determining not only how to carry it out but in what circumstances it is appropriate in that it may lead to a genuine settlement and not a formula for submission.

It is now time to mention a characteristic of Peace Studies which differentiates the field from others: its positive qualities. Most of those involved in the area do not think of peace as being the mere end of hostility or conflict but a more purposive eventual coming-together for mutual advantage. Thus, Peace Studies must be concerned with approaches to reshaping society and the world order in such a way that not only is violence, overt and covert, eliminated but harmony and co-operation are established and maintained. For this reason, a further dimension is added: the study of the future and possible alternatives to the existing system.

I dream of a world in which we are not separated from each other by fear, suspicion, prejudice or hatred; in which we are free and equal, considerate and loving with each other. By establishing Peace Studies at an intellectual and practical level, we may in some measure help this world to be born. Let us, then, do all we can in the world and in our minds, but above all cherish the humanity in ourselves and in each other, not least in those from whom we are separated by the more superficial barriers of ideology, or religion, or race. Until we can recognise that our common nature and our common destiny are more important than the things which divide us, the shadows will continue to lengthen until night irrevocably falls.

The School of Peace Studies

James O'Connell

It was a Quaker initiative that in 1973 helped to set up at the University of Bradford a university department committed to the study of peace. In British universities at the time, many doubted that peace was a suitable subject for academic study. Also, there were those who objected that such study would be moralistic and out-of-touch with the real world. Hence, the academics at Bradford had to set a doubt at rest and to counter an objection.

In Augustine's great phrase, peace is "the tranquillity of order". To structure the idea and the process of peace for study, the Department of Peace Studies identified five themes of concentration. These are:

1. *Peace theory* Research and teaching deal with the history of peace and the analysis of the concept of peace and related values, especially justice and freedom. In this theme, work is also carried out on nonviolent methods of social change and mediation.

2. *Nuclear and non-nuclear security* Unless the nuclear problem is resolved, there will be both great human evil and the destruction of creation. For that reason the department concentrates a part of its work on the politics, technology, economics and ethics of the nuclear arms race.

3. *Peace and development* In a world grown small, peace studies is concerned to look at global neighbours and at relations between rich and poor countries. Moreover, since 1945 nearly all breakdowns of peace have occurred in the developing world.

4. *Industrialised societies* In this theme, the department has taken up especially the relationship between defence policies, security and economic growth.

5. *Regions in conflict* The choice has been made to specialise in Northern Ireland and the Middle East.

Some comments are in order. Though the nuclear issue has a certain saliency, the more fundamental issue and theme in the department and its more radically innovative work lie in the analysis of peace and nonviolent methods of social change. Unless endeavours are made to change attitudes and values, and to distance states and groups from a traditional and utter reliance on military defence for security, our world will never insulate nuclear weapons from anachronistic views and all that exists will be destroyed.

The department, which has a strong publishing record, has under way research projects that include, among others, the history of peace work, methods of mediation, Soviet and Western nuclear policies, development in Nigeria, economic conversion of defence industries, and the Palestinian uprising. With help from Quaker Trusts, it fosters a most developed effort to train young researchers - there are 24 research students in the department.

The unifying outlook in the department is a concern for peace. This concern is structured intellectually; it is related to the traditional academic disciplines; and it is grounded empirically. Finally, the approach of the department is an applied one and seeks to influence public policy, but it also has a speculative dimension that seeks knowledge for its own sake and with a detachment that safeguards truth.

The Way to Co-operation

Mildred Masheder

Human beings are great co-operators! Why then does this statement so often meet with a certain amount of cynicism in our present society? It is probably because in the world of today we only hear about human aggression and violence and little about our day-to-day co-operative actions, which are still alive in spite of the pressures of a competitive philosophy. Now our survival is once again in question and once more it is only by sheer co-operative effort that we shall be able to overcome together the perils that beset us.

How is it that we have lost so much of our heritage of co-operating? Is it really incompatible with our modern industrial society? Can we come to terms with our competitive culture so that the spirit of co-operation can be nurtured and given an equal place with the individualistic values of today?

We are now at such a turning-point that we have little choice: whether it is the pollution of the planet and the destruction of the rain forests, or the dangers of the increasing proliferation of murderous weapons of war, it is vital that we get together as nations to save ourselves from destruction. It is at least encouraging that there are positive moves in this direction, both on the international scale and the personal.

I shall concentrate on the personal, small-scale approach, which can lay the foundations in young people for larger-scale action when they become adult. I especially appeal to parents to consider all the possibilities of bringing up their children to be able to share and care for others. It is now generally agreed that the basis of these social attitudes is the development of a good concept of self-worth. Only when we feel confident about ourselves can we turn our attention to the needs of others and co-operate with them. This may seem like a contradiction: are we building up the individual at the expense of the group? No, it is patently true that it is the secure, self-reliant person who will be prepared to consider the other's point of view and endeavour to reach agreement.

Children come into the world with an immense zest for life; they are continually creating and, if they are treated with respect and empathy, they will go from strength to strength, feeling that they are doing all right. Of course there must still be boundaries, so that they know the perimeters within which they can operate, and this is the most difficult role of all for parents: to judge where to draw the lines without crushing their children's potential. With very young children, it is well-known that they are unaware of the needs of others, but I believe that too much has been made of their 'egocentric' nature. They can experience positive social activities with their peers as early as the toddler stage and, although they will mostly play on their own with occasional battles over possessions, they are quite capable of co-operating over a joint venture. As they develop the practice of collaboration by working and playing together, this will be reflected in positive attitudes towards others.

This may seem a long way from saving the rain forests, but it is the very basis of future co-operation. There are other components of this process that can start early in life: communication is our basic form of co-operation, and in conflict situations we can learn how to come to some kind of resolution without recourse to violence and physical aggression. Listening is as important as talking in the art of communication, and particular attention is now being paid to what is called active or creative listening, particularly in the area of conflict resolution.

If we can encourage a family life which cherishes the self-regard of all its members, the adults as well as the children, and if communication is fostered by discussions, advocacy and the sorting-out of problems, we are providing a solid foundation for co-operation both inside the home and in the wider world.

This applies equally to the relationship between teachers and their pupils and, indeed, all those concerned with the education and well-being of young children. The more they can introduce co-operative activities and joint collaboration, the more harmonious will be the atmosphere in the classroom. This is not just an idealistic theory: where these approaches of affirmation, good communication and co-operation have been tried systemati-

systematically, they have really worked, with great improvement in relationships and consideration for others. My book *Let's Co-Operate*, for parents and teachers of children aged from three to eleven, gives many activities to follow along these lines.

The revival of co-operative games has played a substantial role in promoting a non-competitive attitude towards play, where no-one is the loser and everybody wins. Some have been traditional games handed down from one generation of child-hood to the next; there are also games from countries all over the world which have retained their heritage of a co-operative way of life.

A consistent approach by the home and school along these lines can help to counter the present free range of competitive-ness to which we are subjected from early childhood. Compe-tition is often the antithesis of co-operation, even if the team spirit can be evoked to counter its worst effects. It is argued that we need competition right from the beginning of our lives in order to face the real world. In fact we are desperately in need of co-operation, in order to be able to change the frightening realities of our present world into the art of living together in peace and harmony.

Community

Cyril Wright

One of the strongest arguments for pacifism is that it involves a way of life consistent with its basic beliefs. Committed pacifists are tested and judged by the way they live. In our divided and wasted world, it has been asked whether it is only the pacifist strain in people that gives community its appeal as a possible solution. We read evidences and confessions of a strong pacifist tendency in all sorts of public figures, not strong enough to make them pacifists, but powerfully influencing attitudes and decisions. This is a source of hope and confidence.

Those who advocate nonviolence, tolerance, peaceful co-existence, love for others and reverence for all life, must be seen to observe - as far as they are able - the same principles towards their neighbours as they wish should be effective among nations. If the practice of peace is the way to peace, then it is constructive and enlightening to have some framework within which, to echo the words of George MacLeod, founder of the Iona Community, "these ideas can be seen to work".

Community is a word which, like communism and communion, stems from the concept of something shared or exchanged. In a wide sense, any group of people, both adults and children, with common aims and interests may be thought of as a community. It may be a family, a play group or something on a larger scale. The wider the circle, the greater the danger of division among its members, and the consequent watering-down of purposes once so firmly adopted. It would be unreal to ignore these hazards.

Community ventures that are mainly escapist are of no significance to the world outside. Co-operative endeavours, commencing as a means of subsistence for objectors to war and materialism, based on crafts or crop production; libertarian residential schools such as Summerhill and Kilquhanity;

educational republics with citizen government like the former Little Commonwealth supervised by Homer Lane; communities depending for their livelihood upon a variety of sources both within and outside the location, will succeed insofar as they mirror in their conduct the principles and relationships which if universally followed would leave no place for war.

Communities usually start with a 'honeymoon' period, of sweetness and light; the difficulties begin when individual differences assert themselves, and it may not be long before this happens. One irony of voluntary communal living is that the very imperfections of social life which people find so distressing and wish to change, follow them into the enclave they have created, and test to the full, even to breaking-point, their pacifist standards. Suspicion, tension, jealousy, competitiveness, and other drives and impulses that feed war, can find their way into community, because we are all subject to them in varying degree.

Much of this fragmentation and impermanence have been overcome in communities founded on a religious basis, with a common form of worship and a devotional stimulus which lifts the members above material conflict. The conjunction of work and prayer, and a deep concern for the world outside, give strength, assurance and stamina to the circle. The Bruderhof, in Sussex, hold that no effort can succeed without "a focal point, a central dynamic, a common conviction, a unity of purpose".

A most desirable aspect of community life is the giving of service, the practical value of which pacifists have been among the first to recognise. The small unit with its modest headquarters in an urban area, where the members are always on call to provide routine or emergency aid to the elderly, infirm or incapable, may be one such useful venture. A few dedicated people living right among the underfed, ill-housed inhabitants of a run-down district, sharing their suffering and providing for them with the co-operation of shopkeepers and artisans, is a way of becoming an integral and caring part of an existing community. A successful instance was the Pacifist Service Units, whose record of rescues and relief during and after air-raids in the Second World War exemplified the spirit of service based on close, understanding relationship. Technical training and an acquired knowledge of people and society were essential for this demanding work. There were about a hundred full-time members, divided into units with common living quarters, taking meals at a common table, and sometimes pooling their own small savings. Ways of continuing and adapting the work to post-war conditions were planned, and in 1948 Family Service Units were set up to promote the welfare of families and groups seriously disadvantaged through lack of personal, social or economic resources.

In their reaching out towards those who do not live among them but who can share their life and discoveries on short visits, there are three communities which may be mentioned. The Taizé Community in France is a centre of attraction for thousands of pilgrims, mostly young people from all over the world. The basic roll of 30 people swells to bursting-point as they are joined by individuals and parties, uniting in praise and intercession in the beautifully-decorated chapel; taking part in discussions on issues of both personal and universal importance, with the overriding theme of reconciliation. Though basically Christian, they welcome visitors of many religious faiths, or of none.

Also in France, the Community of the Ark finally settled on 2,000 acres of land south of the Massif Central. The founder, Lanza del Vasto, visualised a community where there would be politics without violence, production without machines, a society without exploitation, religion without intolerance - a return to the simple life and to craftsmanship. Lanza del Vasto has died, but the spirit of his mission, which received the blessing of Gandhi, continues.

Lower Shaw Farm is a small group in north-east Wiltshire. The members live in accommodation which they or their predecessors have added to old farm buildings, and they cultivate a small area of land on organic principles. A regular programme of events - study sessions; yoga and massage; whole-food cookery; rural celebrations; women's weekends; cycling and gardening, and many others - open the community to local or more distant people. Paradoxically, through its acceptance of a changing personnel, Lower Shaw Farm has acquired stability: a useful lesson in itself.

Few would dispute that the world we live in is motivated strongly by self-interest; and by a craving for security, dependent upon present or threatened violence, and the squandering of vital and often irreplaceable resources. Social regeneration is basic to any improvement. Community living can offer a pattern for an alternative society which does not need war, violence and material extravagance to sustain it.

Lifestyle

Mike Thomas

My grandfather, so I was told, loved to recite verses of poetry, often in public. On one occasion at the beginning of the Second World War, he was giving a public recitation when suddenly the sirens wailed and the hall was plunged into darkness. He continued after only a short pause, until the room flickered to life again amid appreciative applause. I do not know why he did this, nor indeed why he took his fishing rod to France during the First World War. Perhaps both gestures were comments on the insanity of what was happening.

My father joined the Air Force as a cook before the last war. During a short period of leave after serving in Palestine, he married my mother, set me on the way, and was then despatched to France where he died on the 'Lancastria' during the fateful retreat from Dunkirk. I don't think my mother ever quite recovered from the loss.

Unlike my grandfather and my father, my prospects of avoiding direct involvement in a war look good, although I did begin to doubt this as I stood on a dreary Didcot railway station on the day President Kennedy issued his ultimatum as Russian ships, loaded with nuclear missiles, steamed towards Cuba. The rush of a high-speed train caught my breath at this moment of reflection and seemed to herald the approach of the first nuclear fireball. It was not to be. The cold war stayed cold!

The 'third world war' fears of the 1970s have receded, and leaders of all the main political parties are still maintaining that the 'nuclear deterrent' has preserved the peace since Hiroshima and Nagasaki, despite the fact that some 20 million people have been killed in post-war conflicts. This period has also had its share of bestial dictators, such as Idi Amin and Pol Pot, who have tried to outshine Hitler in their sadistic cruelty. At the same time, a 'silent holocaust' has taken place, far greater than that caused by the Nazis. Approximately 30 million people are dying of hunger and hunger-related diseases every year. What are the lessons of history? Whatever they are, we appear not to have learnt from them.

From an early age, the prospect of war did, of course, frighten me. However, it did not surprise me that people should go to war, "there always have been wars and there always will be". What did puzzle me was poverty and starvation. Why were people starving while I had plenty? From time to time, the thought of this would bring me to tears.

As I grew older, I would partly salve my conscience by making donations to Oxfam, but the mystery remained until I reached the age of 41. It was then that I came across a book called *The Future in our Hands* written by a Norwegian, Erik Dammann. The first section of the book described the slave trade, colonial exploitation and some of the advanced civilisations that existed in Africa and South America before the start of the European plunder. The author went on to describe how the present neo-colonial system developed, and how this enables rich industrialised countries to dominate world trade and finance to the disadvantage of the poor, particularly in the so-called Third World.

This revelation came as a great shock to me, particularly as I could see that my ordinary everyday consumer habits heaped coals on the furnace of this system. People work under near-slave conditions in Brazil, Bangladesh, Sri Lanka and Kenya to grow unnecessary cash-crops like tea and coffee to obtain foreign exchange which enables their ruling elites to buy arms, build large dams and hotels, and destroy forests for export-oriented cattle ranching and timber extraction.

Ruling elites, and the majority of consumers in the rich countries, benefit most from this exploitation, whilst the already minute proportion of wealth shared by the world's poor majority decreases every year. Those people who choose to ignore the effects of our affluence on the poor majority would do well to remember that the arms trade and the build-up of our armed forces and nuclear weapons are to maintain our economic advantages and security.

Perhaps most wars throughout history have been fought for economic reasons, using religious or occult ideas where this suits an aggressor's purpose, as one tribe covets the wealth that another tries to secure for itself alone. I therefore argue that neither affluence, nor indeed most of our everyday consumer-actions, can be reconciled with true pacifism. Our lifestyle can in itself be an act of violence.

Each hardwood door we buy, each cigarette we smoke, contributes to desertification. The cosmetics we use may have involved intense animal suffering in their manufacture. Do we stop to consider that investment in High Street clearing-banks means supporting the systems which create poverty? For most people, private cars cannot be considered an essential mode of transport and yet some families have two or three cars. The contribution of cars to lead pollution and acid rain is well known. Money spent on a car is money that is not used to provide, say, 40 substantial homes for poor tribal families in India. Grain imported from poor countries to feed our cattle and domestic pets is grain that is not distributed to those who are starving. Do you follow the drift of the argument?

I am pleased to say that the book *The Future in our Hands* led to the formation of a non-religious, non-party-political move-ment of the same name, with branches in 16 different countries. The greatest support for the movement is in Scandinavia, where there are 30,000 members. The movement in Norway has become influential and is currently engaged in a ten-year study - funded by the Norwegian parliament - to consider alternative futures for Norway, taking into account more ethical trading arrangements with poor countries, and development processes which are sus-tainable and environmentally benign. The movement has put the leaders of the main political parties 'on trial' in television pro-grammes, with respect to their record on world poverty and environmental issues. The movement is non-hierarchical and non-dogmatic, preferring to lay the emphasis on the need for human values such as sharing, co-operation, fellowship, truth, compassion and nonviolence.

Pacifism surely has to be a way of life that involves more than just a willingness to 'turn the other cheek'. Even if we find it quite impossible to respond to everything our consciences dictate, is that any excuse for doing nothing?

Vegetarianism

Swindon Pulse Wholefood Co-Op

Why include an article on vegetarianism in a book about pacifism? The links between pacifism and vegetarianism are not about being right-on or trendy: they're about caring for ourselves and other people, and sustaining healthy life on our planet; a way of seeing the human race as one part of an intricately woven web of life on earth, and having respect towards everything living. Ethically, both vegetarianism and pacifism are intent upon nonviolence, towards people and animals. If it is wrong to assume the power to take human life, individually as murder or *en masse* in war, then surely it is also wrong to take upon oneself the right to kill an animal.

Of course it's difficult to argue morals, and everyone has their own guide-lines, but there are plenty of other ways to point out how wasteful, cruel and unnecessary a meat- and dairy-led diet is. Nutritionally, people do not need animal protein in order to eat a healthy and balanced diet. By using alternative sources like beans, pulses, grains and nuts that are cheaper and healthier, vegetarians and vegans get all the protein they need without the fat or the synthetic hormones and antibiotics used in modern intensive livestock farming. In recent times, the horrendously damaging effects of the agriculture industry - damaging to the quality of its product, its consumer and its environment - has become all too clear. Examples include livestock fed on diseased meat and passing infection on to humans; vast amounts of animal slurry polluting streams and rivers; salmonella in eggs; milk full of a frightening cocktail of chemicals. Not the most healthy way to eat!

There has also been much recently in the Press about the disgusting, inhumane and unhygienic state of British slaughterhouses, and that doesn't take into the account the effect such horror must have on the people who work in them - do they, as soldiers in wars must, become desensitised to the stench of blood and death and the sound of shrieks and squeals that are, after all, not so different from a scene of mass human slaughter?

Like pacifism, vegetarianism makes ecological sense. The meat-producing industry is incredibly wasteful of natural resources - vegetable protein that could be eaten directly by people is fed to animals that are then slaughtered and eaten; with the result that it takes five times as much land to feed meat-eaters as it does vegetarians. Economically, it is the poorer nations of the world that suffer most - while the West feeds its livestock largely on vegetable protein imported from Third World countries, millions of people there starve,and food shortages increase the likelihood of war, of increased arms spending, of ever-spiralling national debt.

Taking a choice to live as a vegan - avoiding animal products for food, clothing and other consumer goods - seems to be a logical step once one has decided not to support any aspect of the meat industry. Dairy farming is closely interlinked with beef and veal: in order to lactate, a cow has to have recently given birth so, while we drink its milk, every calf becomes a by-product of the industry, to be killed at the age of a few months. Dairy herds are kept in confined conditions (to maximise profit), hence they are prone to infection which is treated with routine doses of antibiotics. This is the supposedly natural food that we are encouraged to consume by the pinta. It is, of course, naturally designed for calves, not people, which is why we find it difficult to digest with its excessive fat content, leading to stomach disorders and various allergies. Eggs are also a health risk, even when they are salmonella-free, being a high source of cholesterol and fat. The battery-cage system of egg production is barbaric, keeping hens for their whole lives in 20-inch-wide cages where they are unable to spread their wings, peck in the ground for food or make a dust bath. Even free-range production means that, of all the eggs hatched for future layers, some 50% yield male birds which are therefore useless and have to be killed. Thus to eat any dairy produce is to contribute directly to the profit and the cruelty of the meat industry.

Vegetarianism and pacifism are both principles put into practice. They are about people in a takeaway age reclaiming the power of choice over what they do, and about how exercising that choice can affect the world. Having started to think about what you eat, you can make certain decisions and use your power as a consumer or a producer to work towards safer, healthier and fairer methods of food production and consumption. Likewise, you can decide that co-operation and compromise are more positive ways of dealing with conflict than aggression. Just as war is senseless, destructive and undeniably harmful, so the unnecessary and widespread slaughter of animals for human consumption is ecologically and economically short-sighted, bad for people's health, animals' welfare and global resources.

Alternative Technology

Roger Kelly

It is significant that the biblical metaphor of beating swords into ploughshares uses technology to symbolise the change from warfare to pacifism, because it shows the extent to which technology has been and still is at the root of aggression. The multinational military-industrial complex is simply the most recent manifestation of how human resources have been poured into military-technological research, justified on the one hand by 'security' and on the other by 'spin-off' into material improvements to the human condition. We are constantly being fed the argument that, but for this dependence of civil on military technology, we would all live impoverished and somehow less humane lives when the opposite is patently true.

So what is the alternative? A technology which is rooted in and inspired by a love for life in its wholeness, for the planet as a living organism within which humanity has a heavy responsibility for its intervention in the flow of natural forces. A technology which is energised by a burning desire to understand and work in harmony with this flow of forces. A technology which returns to the fundamental needs of humanity and seeks to meet those needs in every human being as a basic right, while still respecting the needs of the whole earth organism.

The industrial nations have chosen a technology of food production which treats the earth's surface as the floor of a chemical works where food is 'engineered' with huge inputs of mainly oil-based chemicals and fossil-fuelled machinery, in total disregard of the ecology of human, animal and plant communities. The food thus produced is then transported, using yet more fossil fuels, sometimes to the opposite side of the globe, to satisfy the desires of the rich at the expense of the needs of the poor. The technological challenge here is to marry the traditional agricultural community's deep-rooted understanding of the sustainable food-growing potential in each unique patch of earth with the demands of a human population vast in numbers, increasingly mobile and in need of diverse sources of nourishment.

We have become dependent on energy systems which extract non-renewable resources from the earth's crust, then burn them with catastrophic effect on the planet's health; or in the case of nuclear power convert them via processes whose inherent dangers require the unattainable human infallibility. We are striving, rightly or wrongly, for ever further extensions of the human body and mind, but in our haste are refusing to examine the violence done to the planet in the process. We have to humbly acknowledge and work towards an understanding of the vast natural energy flows which sustain life on earth - the solar, wind, hydro, tidal and wave harnessing devices we have now are only first steps on a ladder of sustainable energy technology.

These two examples of how we have failed to meet simple human needs because of attitudes of conflict instead of co-operation show the extent of the challenge before us. We have to start now to question all our assumptions about technology - why we need it, how we use it and on what basis we decide its direction - if the planet is to survive our onslaught.

Alternatives

Ruth Leger Sivard

Governments must continually make choices in the allocation of public funds. The decisions are seldom made in terms of a simple weighing of alternatives, particularly as between military defence and the public's welfare.

Protection, for example, comes in various forms. At present, one government in three spends more on weapons than on schools; two in three spend more to guard against external enemies than against all the threats to health and well-being that people face in their daily lives.

In this lop-sided world, it is time that the public in every nation was given an official annual accounting of how its money is being spent, what choices had to be made, and why. No flim-flam, no obfuscation, just a straightforward report to the taxpayer that lays it all out.

Pending the real thing, we must make do with pieces of the jigsaw puzzle (see below). Can a nation really afford to buy another aircraft carrier if it cannot feed all its people, or to spend generously on Star Wars research when it has so little to invest against the AIDS epidemic? If the decision-makers have the answers to such questions, why are they not on the public record?

COSTS OF PROTECTION

Weapons		Other Options
50 MX 'Peacekeepers'	=	Year's cost of US health programme for long-term home care of about 1 million chronically-ill children and elderly.
Research on Star Wars (*fiscal year 1988*)	=	An elementary school education for 1,400,000 children in Latin America.

1 aircraft carrier (Nimitz class)	= 1 solid meal a day for 6 months for the 20 million Americans who do not get enough to eat.
1 Trident submarine	= 5-year programme for universal child immunisation against 6 deadly diseases, preventing 1 million deaths a year.
1 Trafalgar submarine	= Cost to UK public of fee of £10 for sight tests and £3 for dental tests, formerly paid by national health insurance.
2 frigates (F 30)	= Cost of campaign for global eradication of smallpox, which created annual savings 10 times the investment.
1-year operating cost of anti-submarine warfare cruiser	= Housing for 1 year for three-quarters of homeless families in London.
2 fighter aircraft (JA 37)	= Installation in Third World of 300,000 hand pumps to give villages access to safe water.
1 tanker aircraft (VC 10)	= 4 years of UK research on AIDS at current levels of government spending.
2 infantry combat vehicles	= Year's supply of nutrition supplements for 5,000 pregnant women at risk.
10 anti-tank missiles	= Trained guide-dogs for some of the 146,000 blind people in the UK.
1-hour operating cost of a B-1 bomber	= Community-based maternal health care in 10 African villages to reduce maternal deaths by half in a decade.
9mm personal defence weapon (military pistol)	= Year's supply of vitamin A capsules for 1,000 pre-school children at risk.

PEACEMAKERS

*Some people who have explored
nonviolent ways of working for peace*

Gandhi

Tony Augarde

Mohandas Karamchand Gandhi was born in 1869 in Porbandar, an Indian seaside-town north of Bombay. In 1888 he came to Britain to study law. Here he read some of the Bible for the first time and was particularly impressed by the Sermon on the Mount with its advice to "resist not evil".

He returned to India in 1891 to work as a lawyer but he was unsuccessful because he was shy, yet unwilling to be pushed about. So in 1893 he took a job in South Africa, representing the interests of Indian merchants. Shortly after reaching South Africa, he experienced its racial prejudice when he was ejected from a first-class railway compartment because a white man objected to him being there, even though Gandhi had a first-class ticket.

Gandhi joined with his fellow-Indians in working for their rights, and it was in this struggle that he developed the nonviolent techniques he was to use later in India. He opposed unfair taxes levied on Indian workers and he agitated to get Indians their voting rights. In 1904 he set up Phoenix Farm outside Johannesburg, a community where he started to practise simple community living, which he continued at a new community, Tolstoy Farm, five years later.

In 1907 he began a campaign against the laws that made Indians register if they wanted to live in South Africa. 3,000 Indians publicly burnt their registration cards. Another great demonstration against racial discrimination took place in 1913, when Gandhi got a contingent of Indian women to march illegally over the border from the Transvaal into the Natal coalfields, where they persuaded the miners to go on strike. When Gandhi and the miners were savagely punished, the outcry made Prime Minister Smuts negotiate with Gandhi, and this resulted in the Indian Relief Act of 1914 which removed some of the burdens from Indians. Gandhi was now convinced of the power of non-violent disobedience to make people aware of injustices.

Gandhi returned to India, an experienced political campaigner. He set up a new community, an 'ashram' at Ahmedabad. People living at the ashram had to be nonviolent and truthful, had to do farming and spinning for their living, and have no servants or personal possessions. At the ashram, women enjoyed full freedom and equal rights, there was complete religious tolerance, and caste distinctions were ignored.

Gandhi became involved in campaigns helping the Indian people. The salt march of 1930 is a good example of Gandhi's nonviolence, or *satyagraha* he called it (from *satya* truth and *graha* strength). To protest at the government's salt tax, Gandhi proposed a 240-mile march from Ahmedabad to the coastal town of Dandi. The salt tax charged the Indian people for a basic human necessity and prevented them making their own salt. Gandhi wrote to the Viceroy, Lord Irwin, explaining his intentions: ''My ambition is no less than to convert the British people through nonviolence, and thus make them see the wrong they have done to India''.

When the marchers reached the sea, they started making salt from the sea-water, thus breaking the law. This gesture led to civil disobedience breaking out in many parts of India. 60,000 people were arrested.

The second stage of the campaign was to try and take over the salt works at Dharasana. Volunteers marched towards the salt works and, as policemen struck them down with heavy sticks, more volunteers came forward to take their place. Although thousands more arrests were made, the Viceroy decided it was a stalemate and he held talks with Gandhi, which resulted in the Salt Acts being interpreted more humanely and in an agreement that Gandhi could represent his Congress Party at the 1931 Round Table Conference in London. The Conference led nowhere but the salt march gave Indians self-respect and confidence that they could gain independence.

India finally became independent in 1947 but Gandhi was

unhappy with the settlement because it divided India into two states - India and Pakistan - the first largely for Hindus, the second largely for Muslims. Gandhi did his best to pacify the violence between Hindus and Muslims and his work achieved some success. But in 1948 he was shot and killed by a fellow Hindu who believed Gandhi was betraying the Hindus by working for reconciliation.

In the years following independence, the Government led by Nehru (Gandhi's former disciple) ignored Gandhi's schemes for revitalising the villages. Instead they concentrated on industrialisation, which Gandhi saw was not the answer to India's problems. India has a huge population and therefore no shortage of workers; industrialisation only makes unemployment worse by replacing humans with machines. Gandhi's answer lay in India's 500,000 villages, which could be small, self-sufficient, democratic units.

In advocating self-sufficiency, grass-roots democracy, smallness and simple living, Gandhi anticipated by several decades the 'small is beautiful' ideas which are now increasingly respected. Similarly, he was a pioneer in pressing for the equality of women, in stressing the value of mixing manual work with intellectual work, and in his progressive ideas about education.

Gandhi's political and social philosophy has been unjustly neglected. He is better known for his nonviolence or *satyagraha*, which has been very influential even though it has sometimes been misunderstood. *Satyagraha* is not simply a strategy for opposing evil without using violence - it is a whole way of reconstructing society, using love and striving for truth.

Gandhi said: "To me, Truth is God and there is no way to find Truth except the way of nonviolence". Violence separates people, but the search for truth is a communal enterprise in which we have to work *together*.

Satyagraha uses nonviolent resistance to make one's opponent face up to the fact of injustice or exploitation. However, while *satyagrahis* use various nonviolent methods to confront or persuade an opponent - methods like sit-downs and sit-ins, strikes, fasts, demonstrations, boycotts, picketing and non-cooperation (all of which Gandhi used) - they should also be doing constructive work to improve the situation. Every time Gandhi started a campaign against some injustice, he also started constructive schemes to improve conditions.

Albert Einstein said that Gandhi's great contribution to our time was his determination to moralise politics. Gandhi insisted that you can apply the same moral values to politics, business or industry as you do in private life. Love, truth, nonviolence - all these ideals can be applied here and now to every aspect of life. ''It is perfectly possible'', as Gandhi said, ''for an individual to adopt this way of life without having to wait for others to do so''.

Martin Luther King

Cyril Wright

On 1 January 1863, while the American Civil War was at its height, President Lincoln issued the Emancipation Proclamation whereby all slaves in the rebel states should be free. In 1866, when the war had ended, the Civil Rights Act was passed, guaranteeing the rights of all citizens, regardless of race and colour.

Yet, in spite of their defeat in the war, the owners of the cotton and tobacco plantations in the South had no intention of accepting the principle of equality between Whites and Blacks. Most Blacks, after emancipation, had to work for their former owners. Enforced by the so-called "Jim Crow Laws" passed by the Southern states, there was racial segregation in restaurants, on trains and buses, in hospitals and schools, even in prisons and homes for the blind. Harsh discrimination against the Black citizens hardened and continued into the present century, with lynching and other intimidation from groups such as the Ku Klux Klan.

At this time, a man was growing up who was to lead the struggle for Blacks and Whites to enjoy equal rights and benefits. Martin Luther King was born in 1929, at Atlanta in the Southern state of Georgia, the son of a Baptist preacher. The family was comfortably off, but young Martin knew what segregation meant when he had to leave his White friends and attend a school for Black children. He became interested in the teachings of Mahatma Gandhi and his advocacy of nonviolence. Martin became a minister in Montgomery, Alabama.

It was in Montgomery, in 1955, that the first challenge to White supremacy occurred when Rosa Parks, a Black seamstress, refused to give up her seat on a bus to a White passenger. She was arrested and fined. Martin Luther King took action. The Black people agreed to boycott the buses, and walk, ride on mules or drive wagons to work. Supporters from all over the world gave money to provide a pool of cars, and the boycott continued for 11 months, during which time King's house was bombed.

"My wife and baby are all right", he said to the angry crowds. "I want you to go home and put down your weapons. We cannot solve this problem through retaliatory violence. We must meet violence with nonviolence . . . we must meet hate with love".

This was the keynote of Martin Luther King's leadership. In 1956, the United States Supreme Court ordered an end to segregation. It was a victory not only for Montgomery but for all the states where the Blacks were persecuted. Dr King widened the protest up and down the country, increasing his influence and inspiring thousands to march for the cause. He was physically attacked, and several times arrested. The rallying song, "We Shall Overcome!" was often heard at his demonstrations.

The pressure culminated in the Great March of 100,000 on Washington in 1963, and the Civil Rights law was eventually passed in 1964.

Subsequent efforts by Martin Luther King were less successful, and he became unpopular for his opposition to the Vietnam War. At Memphis he intervened in support of a strike of garage-workers. On April 4th 1968, while standing on a balcony in that town with some of his close acquaintances, he was shot by an assassin's bullet.

He had been awarded, in 1964, the Nobel Prize for Peace. It was a fitting tribute to a man who had declared "Nonviolence is a powerful and just weapon. It is a weapon unique in human history, which cuts without wounding and ennobles the person who wields it".

Danilo Dolci

Cyril Wright

Danilo Dolci was born in Trieste in 1924, the son of a station-master. His mother came from Yugoslavia. He developed a love of music and literature, but gave up the idea of a remunerative career, because he wanted to work for a better world. He re-sisted fascism and military service, and developed pacifist views. His work in a Christian community of children left homeless by the Second World War, taught him the value of life in a group. One day he asked himself, ''What about the rest of the world?''

His travels took him to the island of Sicily, where much was happening in defiance of Italian law. The Mafia, sworn to defy all established forms of justice, had matters under their control; the police and some high-ranking politicians not daring to cross their path for fear of the consequences. The working people were poor and badly housed. Sanitation was inadequate; there was much disease and little employment. No wonder that Dolci de-scribed the region as ''one of the most miserable and blood-drenched areas in the world''.

He felt that it was his first duty to get the people to realise that things could improve. They were idle because no work was made available to them, and this in an island badly needing roads, schools and houses. In 1956, Danilo and some friends decided to put their ideas into practice. The workers could not withdraw their labour since they had no work. Near the small town of Partinico there was an old bridle-path in need of repair. A hundred men were persuaded to work on it, unpaid and without permission. They were equipped only with their working tools. Within ten minutes, police arrived and ordered the work to stop. Danilo refused, but held out his hand as a gesture of friendship. This was refused and he was arrested. He sat on the ground in imitation of Mahatma Gandhi, whereupon the officers roughly carried him away.

In the Court Room, Dolci declared: "Not to ensure work for all in accordance with the Constitution is to commit murder". He was sentenced to four months' imprisonment, but what he called "the strike in reverse" - and other actions, such as fasting - drew attention to children dying of hunger and to the need for public works, such as a reservoir. He helped to form study groups and action centres where people could get information of what was needed in their district.

Interest, concern and indignation spread over Europe. The Danilo Dolci Trust was formed, and one of its first projects was the building of a new school in Partinico, with facilities for both children and parents.

During his years in Sicily, Dolci has consistently opposed all Mafia activities, which he sees as a most pernicious form of social oppression and one of the major causes of backwardness in Sicily. He has collected evidence of Mafia activity throughout Sicily and fearlessly exposed it: an action which forced the Italian government to set up an Anti-Mafia Commission.

Although the Mafia rules by intimidation and violence, Danilo will never use violence himself. In his 1960 book *Spreco* ("Waste"), he denounces violence as a means of overcoming injustice or of balancing the violence of the Mafia. Like Gandhi and Martin Luther King, he has found new weapons in the struggle for right against wrong - methods such as fasting, demonstrations and co-operative action.

In 1956, though not a Communist, he was awarded the Lenin Peace Prize, and in 1968, an honorary degree from the University of Berne. He served as Vice-Chair of the War Resisters' International. He is truly known as "the Gandhi of Sicily".

Tolstoy

Ronald Sampson

Tolstoy's greatness is so many-sided that it is not easy to pin-point his unique stature. I would cite the depth of his love of humanity, his detestation of and absolute fearlessness in the presence of Power, his unquenchable devotion to the truth whatever the cost in personal suffering. As he lay dying at Astapova railway station in 1910, an old man of 82, among his last words were "I do not know what it is that I have to do . . . " and again, "I have so loved the truth . . . " His anguish derived from the knowledge that, despite his efforts to save people from their terrible fate, he could not persuade more than a handful to listen. Even today, more than a hundred years after he wrote it, the brilliant and searching analysis of our social pathology contained in *War and Peace*, and in the second epilogue in particular, is still either despised or ignored. The fact that his dire predictions have been so rapidly fulfilled does not seem to predispose us to listen more attentively to what he had to say.

Tolstoy is first and last a profoundly religious thinker, and was accordingly excommunicated by the Orthodox Church. Because Tolstoy's religion was profound, it can be expressed very simply. All people are equal in that they owe their lives and their duty to the common author of their being, whom Tolstoy called God. It is His will that all his creatures should do good to one another and under all circumstances abstain from evil. All people are in an identical situation: living their lives, from which they may be removed at any moment and for ever, among other people like themselves. The time therefore for love, compassion, humility, understanding is *now*, for tomorrow I may cease to be. To punish or injure a fellow human under any circumstances is to forget that no-one is equipped to judge the degree of responsibility of another, and that an injury to another is automatically an injury to my own best self.

Given the irreducible simplicity of his ethical teaching, clear and unmistakeable to all, it followed that he had little sympathy with any abstruse theology or theories of political obligation, which he saw as designed to confuse and deceive common people concerning their otherwise simple and self-evident duties to help one another.

Tolstoy's art arises out of, and is illuminated by, his religious philosophy. It may seem purely arbitrary to select anything for discussion in a few words from his works, novels, tales, plays, which are as rich and all-embracing as life itself. Yet central to all Tolstoyan thought is the supreme value of forbearance and forgiveness, with the corollary that the will to dominate and get one's own back is morally crippling. This is the central theme of tales like *God Sees the Truth but Waits* and *Master and Man*. The same theme provides some of the most moving episodes in his greatest works, *War and Peace*, *Anna Karenina*, and *Resurrection*: Prince Andrei, mortally wounded at Borodino, catching up at last with his hated enemy Anatole Kuragin, himself at the point of death under the surgeon's amputating knife; Vronsky and Karenin, the lover and the husband brought together at the foot of Anna's bed, where she is thought to be dying in childbirth of puerperal fever; Prince Nekhlyudov seeking forgiveness of Katusha Maslova, the maid who he had grievously wronged.

The root of the evil in humans can be expressed in many different ways. Tolstoy, in attempting to define the source of human suffering, placed his chief emphasis on the alleged right of self-defence. This 'right' he held to be spurious and rejected. In so far as defending my body involves doing injury to another, I do something I know to be wrong. In so far as I do not return good for evil, I do myself an injury as well. While other people may destroy my body, which is in any event mortal and perishable, they cannot injure my essential self, my integrity. This is indestructible, except in so far as I myself destroy it. This is clearly understood by those in power. Hence the lengths to which they have gone in every generation to rob heretics of their integrity. A heretic's life is normally only taken in desperation after all attempts to destroy that integrity have failed. Those in power have the ultimate sanction; heretics, if their will does not break, have the ultimate triumph, but not a triumph as the term is commonly understood. As soon as I depart from this metaphysic, I open the way for the justification of an apparatus, an organisation whose an organisation whose alleged purpose is the securing of my defence. Control of this organisation then becomes the vital key in the struggle for power between people; and in this lethal struggle the ripples spread wider and wider until logically all humanity will inevitably be threatened. This has now come about more quickly than even Tolstoy could have foreseen.

The only remedy, Tolstoy insisted, is to teach people by example and clarity of mind that the profession of arms is an evil profession. A murderer at least commits that crime in a meaningfully significant personal context.

The soldier, on the other hand, pursues a profession in which one is bound by oath to obey unconditionally orders to kill at random, men, women and children indiscriminately - people whom he does not even know and with whom he can have no quarrel. This inevitably leads to brutalisation of the soldiers and is productive of great ceaseless atrocities. The most evil of all our social institutions is therefore the oath of allegiance to the Crown or the State.

The only remedy is an ancient one but it is a sufficient one. "Swear not at all . . . let your communication be, Yea, yea; Nay, nay".

Vera Brittain

Harry Mister

During the Second World War, the combination of pacifists, left-wingers, writers and churchpeople became the only opposition to the national coalition in power. They tried to stop the war, they campaigned under considerable difficulties against its barbarities, they fought for the right of dissent and, even before the horrific culmination at Hiroshima, they were pressurising public opinion and government to negotiate a peace that would bring down the fascists, save the people, feed the starving millions of occupied Europe and speed colonial liberation.

No-one played a more committed part in all this than the author Vera Brittain, who died in 1970. The pacifist cause dominated her life from 1937 onwards, when she joined Canon Dick Sheppard as one of the sponsors of the then soaring Peace Pledge Union, of which she was to become Chairperson after the war.

Her grim experience as a VAD nurse in the First World War, and the tragic loss of both her brother and fiancé in that war, left her with an unshakeable commitment to the peace cause. *Testament of Youth*, her autobiography published in 1933, greatly influenced the post-war generations and was outstandingly the most successful of her many books. Her eloquence as both writer and speaker inspired the peace movement before, during and after the Hitler war, just as in the 1920s it had helped to put the League of Nations Union on the map in Britain.

An ardent feminist, she campaigned for women's rights in general, and for their equal right to higher education at a time when few places were available for women at universities. Indian freedom was another cause which she supported, and she related these issues inextricably to her pacifism: "The struggle against war, which is the final and most vicious expression of force, is fundamentally inseparable from feminism, socialism, slave emancipation and the liberation of subject races''.

Peace people of the 1940s will remember her splendid fortnightly *Letter to Peace Lovers*, a personal publishing venture through the war years which did much to sustain anti-war workers and stimulate humanitarian alternatives to the destruction and tragedy of those days. At that time she joined George Bell, Bishop of Chichester, and Corder Catchpool in forming the Bombing Restriction Committee, which campaigned against the saturation bombing of densely-populated German cities, such as the notorious raid on Dresden.

Vera Brittain also played a leading part in the Peace Pledge Union's Famine Relief Campaign, which worked vigorously to get food to the peoples of occupied Europe, starving because of the Allied blockade. This campaign led after the war to the Save Europe Now movement, organised by Victor Gollancz, Vera Brittain, Richard Acland and others, and ultimately to bodies like Oxfam and War on Want, which still spearhead the attack on world poverty.

She welcomed the emergence of CND and the Committee of 100, and showed a very practical concern for people jailed for their activities with the Direct Action Committee. I remember her in 1961 arriving indignantly and a little out of breath at the mammoth Committee of 100 occupation of Trafalgar Square and the surrounding area. She could not find the centre of this vast demonstration and so had sat down on her own in the middle of Whitehall, only to be very politely refused arrest by an avuncular police officer. She was then approaching 70.

George Lansbury

Cyril Wright

In the middle of the last century, there grew up in London's East End a man who, through his work to alleviate poverty and improve opportunities for the working people of Britain, and by his striving for world peace, fully exemplified the title of this book.

George Lansbury, affectionately known as 'G.L.', was twice imprisoned: for acting in solidarity with the suffragettes and, as a councillor in Poplar, for refusing to levy rates on the poor to subsidise the rich.

Peace, however, was his earliest love, and at the age of 11 he silenced his elders with concern over the Franco-Prussian War. At the turn of the century, he braved the jingoist patriotism of the Boer War to stand in the 'khaki election' as a socialist, denouncing the war as wicked. Eventually elected as an MP ten years later, he raised in the House the prosecution of the authors of a *'Don't Shoot'* leaflet addressed to soldiers. Having resigned his seat to stand unsuccessfully as a 'Suffragette' candidate, he became editor of the *Daily Herald* in time to publish the headline "War is Hell" at the outbreak of the First World War. The most significant paper of opposition to the war, and of support for pacifism and conscientious objection, the *Herald* said at the end of the war that it could think of nothing but that the killing was over.

Lansbury returned to Parliament in 1923 and was Leader of the Labour Party from 1931 to 1935. However, at a time when the prospect of war seemed likely, he was ousted amid the clamour of other politicians for rearmament.

Uncompromising in his pacifism and undeterred by ridicule from fellow MPs, he embarked on an arduous series of visits, under the name Embassies of Reconciliation, in which he talked not only to the heads of almost every democratic government in Europe but also to the heads of state in the Balkans and even Hitler and Mussolini. He went to President Roosevelt in the USA.

155

He never gave up hoping that by talking to each other, ideally in formal conference, the world's leaders could avert war. Though this was not to be, his influence did secure the release of a few political prisoners in the totalitarian states. When the war began, he supported the attempt by Queen Wilhelmina of the Netherlands and King Leopold of the Belgians to get the belligerents to negotiate.

George Lansbury served as Chair of the No More War Movement, President of the War Resisters' International, and to the child refugees from Spain and central Europe rescued by the WRI he was known as 'Grandfather George'. Dick Sheppard, founder of the Peace Pledge Union, named him "Public Pacifist Number One" and, fittingly at the time of his death in 1940 at the age of 81, he was PPU President.

In his last message to the PPU he wrote: "Our gospel is as old, true and solid as the hills. Violence and force have been tried again and again, and have always failed because such action is based on the foolish belief that evil may be overcome by evil . . . We are standing foursquare for the principle that all peoples of the world are equal in the sight of God . . . So, comrades, with confidence hold on to the truth your conscience reveals to you, and honour and respect those whose conscience leads them along the opposite road".

6. PACIFIST ORGANISATIONS

The main pacifist groups, and other organisations working for peace

Peace Pledge Union

The Peace Pledge Union was founded in the mid-thirties by the Revd Dick Sheppard, famous not only for his sermons - which were the first ever to be broadcast - but for his sympathetic understanding for all kinds of people, especially the deprived and the underdog. He had been an army chaplain in the First World War and it was from there, caught up with the suffering inflicted by one person on another, that he became convinced that war was incompatible with Christianity, humanity and good sense.

In October 1934, he sent a letter to the Press, saying: "It seems essential to discover whether or not it be true, as we are told, that the majority of thoughtful men in this country are now convinced that war of every kind or for any cause, is not only a denial of Christianity but a crime against humanity, which is no longer to be permitted by civilised people". He invited men who had so far been silent, to send him a postcard saying that they supported the resolution to "renounce war, and never again, directly or indirectly, support or sanction another". Within two days, 2,500 men responded, and in the next few months the number grew to over 30,000.

The resolve to "renounce war" became the basis for the Peace Pledge Union, the name adopted in 1936, when women were also invited to join. The PPU is open to pacifists of all religions and none, and it is not associated with any political party.

Dick Sheppard died suddenly in 1937, just after he had won the Glasgow University Rectorship as a pacifist candidate, defeating Winston Churchill and J B S Haldane. A large sum of money was subscribed to set up a memorial, and a London property was acquired in Endsleigh Street which was named Dick Sheppard House and is still the PPU's headquarters.

Despite some resignations on the outbreak of the Second World War, the number of signatories continued to rise to a peak of 136,000 in April 1940. The PPU continued its opposition to the war, campaigning for such things as the cessation of intensive bombing of German cities and the lifting of the blockade of food imports to Europe. The Central Board for Conscientious Objectors had its office at Dick Sheppard House, and the PPU set up the Pacifist Service Bureau to help COs and others find socially useful work.

After the war, the PPU campaigned for humanitarian treatment of the defeated countries and prisoners of war. It continued campaigning against conscription until compulsory military service was ended in 1960. The Peace Pledge Union also began to study nonviolent resistance, which led to a group called Operation Gandhi that undertook the first civil disobedience demonstration against the atomic bomb and the first demonstration at Aldermaston Atomic Weapons Research Establishment - both in 1952.

More recently, the PPU has been concerned with the Falklands War and the ongoing conflict in Northern Ireland, as well as joining other groups in 1974 in setting up the Campaign against Arms Trade.

The PPU's current campaigns include a Peace Education Project, work on the subject of Children and War, and campaigns centred around Remembrance, including promoting the white poppy as an alternative symbol of peace. The Peace Pledge Union publishes a regular magazine, *The Pacifist*. Members of the PPU are linked with pacifists throughout the world by its affiliation to the War Resisters' International.

Peace Pledge Union, Dick Sheppard House, 6 Endsleigh Street, London WC1H 0DX (telephone 071-387-5501).

Fellowship of Reconciliation

The Fellowship of Reconciliation (FOR) is an ecumenical Christian pacifist movement which began at a conference in Cambridge, England, in the last days of 1914, as a response to the challenge of the First World War. The founders agreed on a statement declaring that as Christians "we are forbidden to wage war" and are called instead to "a life-service for the enthronement of Love in personal, commercial and national life". In 1919 a further conference established the International FOR, which now has members all over the world, though there are as yet no organised branches in Eastern Europe.

In some countries, notably the USA, the FOR basis has been widened to include pacifists of other faiths - for example, Jews and Buddhists - but in England it has remained a specifically Christian movement. In Latin America it takes the form of a continent-wide federation of movements for peace and non-violent liberation called Servicio Paz y Justicia. In the Philippines, it was largely nonviolent training input from International FOR members which inspired and guided the upsurge of 'people power' and the overthrow of the Marcos regime.

In England the membership declined steadily until the 1980s, but more recently there has been a considerable transformation, with less emphasis on the old "conscientious objector image" and more on justice, liberation, nonviolent direct action and inter-faith dialogue. While the original 'Basis' remains as the historic foundation document, a new declaration of principles was agreed which affirms the supremacy of love in human relationships and the equality of all people before God; is committed to the renunciation of war and violence, support for nonviolent movements for justice and liberation and opposition to racism, sexism and other denials of human equality; and calls for lives motivated by service to others rather than by the pursuit of security and comfort or power and privilege.

The FOR publishes a quarterly journal of articles, comment and reviews - *Reconciliation Quarterly*, a bimonthly newsletter *Peacelinks*, a series of briefing papers on a range of topics, and other pamphlets and leaflets from time to time. It encourages regional and group activity and arranges national conferences, exhibitions and acts of witness, often in co-operation with other peace movements. It has links with various denominational pacifist fellowships, is closely linked with national FORs in Ireland, Scotland and Wales, and is affiliated to the War Resisters' International as well as to International FOR.

Fellowship of Reconciliation, 40-46 Harleyford Road, Vauxhall, London SE11 5AY (telephone 071-582-9054).

War Resisters' International

"War is a crime against humanity. I am therefore determined not to support any kind of war and to strive for the removal of all causes of war'' - the basis of War Resisters' International (WRI).

Since its foundation in 1921, WRI has had two main concerns: to serve as a solidarity network for people refusing to take part in war and war preparations, and to promote nonviolence to remove the causes of war.

Today, WRI has 54 affiliates based in 25 countries. In several other countries, it has individual members. In 1989, for the first time since the division of Europe into military blocs, it welcomed new affiliates in Eastern bloc countries, and in 1990 expects to gain its first affiliates for some years in South America and Africa.

In addition to existing as an increasingly global anti-militarist network, WRI also launches its own projects:

· a 1968 demonstration in four Warsaw Pact capitals after the invasion of Czechoslovakia;

· Operation Omega to Bangladesh, a nonviolent action project challenging Pakistan's occupation of what was then East Pakistan;

· the international nonviolent march for demilitarisation, crossing frontiers throughout Europe and spreading the practice of nonviolence training and affinity groups;

· promoting personal peace treaties where citizens of hostile countries draw up joint statements declaring that their primary loyalty is to their common values and to solidarity with each other;

· sending a small team to South Africa to support war resisters there.

In addition, WRI organises a range of conferences and seminars. The major event is a Triennial conference: the two most recent were 'Resistance and Reconstruction', held at a Gandhian ashram in India, and 'People's Power: to change the world without weapons' in Finland. In between, there are smaller conferences:

· a series of women's gatherings on the themes of 'feminism and nonviolence' and 'women and militarism' which began in the 1970s;

· seminars on nonviolent social defence;

· a seminar on 'refusing war preparations: conscientious objection and non-cooperation'.

There are regular days for campaigning: on Prisoners for Peace Day, December 1 each year, WRI produces an Honour Roll of imprisoned conscientious objectors and nonviolent activists against war and asks people to send them seasonal cards; on International Conscientious Objection Day, May 15, a focus country is chosen and protests are made in solidarity with the CO movement of that country. Sometimes, there have been days of simultaneous action, such as for Unilateral Disarmament and for Nicaragua's right to self-determination.

Part of WRI's networking function is met by publishing. The bi-monthly WRI *Newsletter,* now incorporated with *Peace News* monthly, has been chosen as the international communication point for the growing number of war tax resistance and peace tax movements. *The Broken Rifle* newssheet gives short and sometimes urgent news items as the need arises, while every six months women active in the WRI produce *WRI Women. War Resistance* is now being revived as an annual review containing some of the best thinking about nonviolence and pacifism from around the world.

WRI's symbol is the broken rifle. From 1923-74 and again since 1981, the international office has been in England - at 55 Dawes Street, London SE17 1EL (telephone 071-703-7189).

The WRI section in the United States is the War Resisters' League, 339 Lafayette Street, New York 10012.

Quaker Peace & Service

Right from Quaker beginnings at the end of the English civil war, the challenging teaching of Jesus to ''love your enemies'' has been taken very seriously. Joining the Religious Society of Friends (Quakers) meant giving up personal weapons in a sword-carrying and violent age.

Friends were, and still are, known for their egalitarian beliefs and practices. When the Commonwealth ended and the monarchy and court were restored, the new establishment feared Quaker influence. To allay this anxiety and plead for toleration, a testimony was drawn up, addressing the king and conveying that he had nothing to fear from the harmless Quakers. Passages written in 1661 are still quoted, one of the best known being ''The Spirit of Christ, which leads us into all truth, will never move us to fight and war against any man with outward weapons, neither for the kingdom of Christ, nor for the kingdoms of the world''.

Today, the Quaker peace testimony is applied in all areas of life: personal, communal, national and international. But a danger for pacifists is always that of complacency: if spiritually-based nonviolence is to influence human affairs, it must be expressed actively.

Quaker Peace & Service (QPS) is the instrument for the Yearly Meetings of Friends in Britain and Ireland to actively express their international concerns. QPS' offices are in London but its work is worldwide, with people serving in Asia, Africa and Latin America, Europe and the Middle East, in education and development, health and human rights programmes which are compatible with the just reconciliation of conflict.

Some QPS work is longstanding, for example support for the United Nations, and East-West reconciliation. In Geneva the Quaker UN Office offers opportunities for diplomats engaged in disarmament, refugees' aid, development and human rights issues to meet informally, with academics, journalists and other visitors who can shed light on subjects of mutual interest. ''You are able to organise meetings like this and everyone wants to come. No one else can do it,'' said a recent participant.

Similarly, the London Diplomats Group has a regular programme, hosted by QPS. In Belfast, Quaker House is a centre for efforts to understand all sides in the Northern Ireland conflict.

Overseas work focuses on trouble spots, and seeks to promote conflict containment and reconciliation while practical work of immediate value is carried out. The Middle East Placement Programme, for example, has enabled teachers, lawyers, medical and other workers to share a deeper awareness of the problems of the region on their return, through further related work, writing and public speaking.

Quaker Peace & Service, Friends' House, Euston Road, London NW1 2BJ (telephone 071-387-3601).

Anglican Pacifist Fellowship

The Anglican Pacifist Fellowship is a varied group of Anglicans united by the belief that our faith in Jesus Christ demands that we reject all war and preparation for war as being fundamentally against the spirit of the Gospel as revealed in Jesus Christ.

Not only do we reject all war, but we also strive positively to build up peace in the world instead of fear.

We work within the Anglican Church to persuade our fellow Christians that pacifism is an essential part of their faith. We work in many ways in the world at large to help bring about peace and understanding.

In particular, we produce literature, hold peace conferences, argue our case in Church circles, support the Week of Prayer for World Peace, and add the APF witness to demonstrations for peace. We also publish a series of short pamphlets for distribution in local churches, at meetings and on stalls.

Becoming a member is an opportunity to join one's witness for peace to that of others, so that together we may help carry the light of Christ's peace into a world darkened by war and violence. Membership is open to all communicant members of the Church of England, or of a church in communion with it, who believe that their Christian faith implies a total rejection of war. Members of the APF receive the newsletter *Challenge* free every two months. There is an annual Summer Conference, and an annual retreat.

Further details about the Anglican Pacifist Fellowship, and membership forms, are available from the Hon Secretary, Revd S G S Hinkes, St Mary's Vicarage, Bayswater Road, Headington, Oxford OX3 9EY (telephone 0865-61886).

The Fellowship Party

The Fellowship Party, the UK's only pacifist political party, in 1955 opposed Labour's conscription policy, Lib-Lab-Tory support for nuclear weapons and US bases and rearming Germany, Japan and Italy. From its anti-nuclear weapons' tests petition eventually emerged CND. Opposing NATO and the Warsaw Pact, racialism and pollution, it sought total disarmament and pooling world resources for all to use, not a capitalist Europe, economically strengthened NATO and greater division between East and West.

It wants non-nuclear power; British industry and agriculture reorganised and decentralised with industrial democracy to serve all, not private profit; a free National Health Service financed through income tax; free education from infancy to university with adequate grants; decentralised government, proportional representation, an elected second House; slum clearance, rebuilding of sewers, canals and faulty roads, hospitals and schools, and enough new homes to rent or buy to end homelessness.

It would strengthen international law, with disputes settled at the International Court at the Hague, and through the UN give developing nations the means to feed themselves. Disarming totally, it would try to lead non-aligned and Commonwealth nations in a Third Group to reconcile capitalist and so-called Communist nations before the arms race ends in war that could destroy humanity.

The Fellowship Party, Woolacombe House, 141 Woolacombe Road, Blackheath, London SE3 8QP (telephone 081-856-6249).

Other Peace Groups

Besides the pacifist organisations listed above, there are many other groups working for peace, although consisting of people who would not necessarily call themselves pacifists.

Pacifists often work in collaboration with this wider peace movement; indeed, some peace groups - like the Peace Tax Campaign and Campaign against Arms Trade - arose from concerns within pacifist organisations like the Peace Pledge Union. Other groups with whom pacifists share mutual objectives include the National Peace Council, the National Council for Civil Liberties, the Women's International League for Peace and Freedom, and Amnesty International.

There are also many peace groups that concentrate on particular issues (such as the Campaign for Nuclear Disarmament and Greenpeace); organisations for special groups of people - like Pax Christi (for Catholics), the Woodcraft Folk (for children) and the Buddhist Peace Fellowship; and groups working in particular areas (like the Corrymeela Community in Northern Ireland).

So the peace movement consists of a very wide range of individuals and groups, too numerous to list here.

Further information is available from the National Peace Council, 29 Great James Street, London WC1N 3ES (telephone 071-242-3228), and comprehensive address lists are included in the *Peace Diary* published annually by Housmans Bookshop, 5 Caledonian Road, King's Cross, London N1 9DX (telephone 071-837-4473). Peace movement activities are regularly reported in *Peace News*, 55 Dawes Street, London SE17 1EL (telephone 071-703 7189).

7. THE FUTURE

How things could be

AD 2050: a Progress Report

Cyril Wright

Some time during the last quarter of the 20th century, a meeting was held at Swindon, Wiltshire, in the Borough of Thamesdown, said to be one of the fastest-growing towns in the United Kingdom. The somewhat ambitious subject of the meeting was *Demilitarisation Project - Thamesdown*. These startling words induced a number of newcomers to join the regular attendance of pacifists and other peace-workers. A large-scale map was on view, with a key to locations marked in red, which were seen to have links with the military. We can now look back at the conditions existing in those days, and review the changes that have already taken place.

In spite of pockets of militarism still resisting the transition to peaceful objectives, readers will be surprised at the extent to which the pursuit of war pervaded civil and industrial life. Take, for example, our Voluntary Services Information Office, formerly the Army Careers Office, which in its day attracted young men and women at a time of high unemployment to a course of training to kill, on the pretext of travelling to interesting places or of learning a trade. Nowadays, the recognition in many countries of a need for services in areas vulnerable to natural disasters, and for the training required by poorer communities to help organise their native or adopted industries, ensures a steady stream of volunteers offering skills and adaptability.

The extensive building near the park, known as the College of International Service, has incorporated the former Territorial Volunteer Army Reserve Centre, where young men were rigorously trained to reinforce the regular army in times of national emergency. The CIS is in fact today an arm of the Royal College of Science, just over the border with Oxfordshire, from whose title the word 'Military' has long since been removed. Many of its staff live within the Borough of Thamesdown, using the original army officers' houses, where the land once occupied by a camp has returned to agricultural use. The change-over at the College, to education for peaceful purposes, has in every way maintained the high quality of teaching, the excellent results and the lively social life of the establishment.

In the large pedestrian area central to Swindon, displays and exhibitions presenting many aspects of the work of the International Aid Services are a frequent feature, often attended by publicity vans bringing pictures and news from centres of activity elsewhere. Readers will find it hard to believe that, on this site, huge self-propelled guns, capable of destroying life and property at a distance of 20 miles, were formerly put on show; children being allowed to climb over them as a way of self-identification, or were encouraged by smiling soldiers in their smart uniforms to examine and handle the smaller weaponry. The sense of pride that children gained from being at the discharging end of these deadly objects is now directed to the inspection of instruments and equipment displayed by Aid and Services Instructors in their distinctive denim strip, promising excitement and adventure in bringing a better life to millions of the world's poorest people.

Look again, when you pause at the Peace Memorial in Town Hall Square. Visitors wonder at the truncated column which stands nearby, preserved for so many years. The Cenotaph (or Empty Tomb) is inscribed with the names of those who were killed ('fell' was the current evasive expression) in the two major wars of the violent 20th century. This was retained as one of the less explicit types of War Memorial, as they were known. Some were designed as much to celebrate victory as to honour the dead, featuring soldiers with fixed bayonets, and identifying with a religion whose God, by siding only with the victors, proved them to be right. Such offensive statuary throughout the country has now been largely removed, together with guns captured from 'the enemy', mines used as collecting boxes, and other barely credible mementoes beloved by the last supporters of militarism. The International Peace Memorial records the courage and initiative of men and women of many nations - nurses, doctors, conservationists, teachers, pacifists - whose efforts have contributed to a caring and sharing world, increasingly free from the threat of war.

One of the largest factories in the area is a branch of one of Britain's most successful makers of optical instruments and medical equipment. They had a long record of alternating between war-products and the making of goods for human needs. It was at a time when the Borough of Thamesdown had declared itself a nuclear-free zone, that this company's contract with the Atomic Weapons Research Establishment at Aldermaston exposed its indifference to a growing climate of opinion. Since the abandonment of nuclear weapons, and the progressive reduction of conventional arms, firms are gradually transferring their work-place and work-force to peaceful production. This in turn has a beneficial effect upon their sub-contractors.

If we look at the communications and educational services in the Borough, the local newspapers had, on the whole, a good record of giving fair expression both to the supporters of militarism and force, and to the advocates of disarmament, non-violence, and aid for the Third World. In our libraries, research students requiring books and magazines on the history and strategy of war, or examples of the vast amount of war fiction that flooded the bookshops in the last century, can no longer find shelves labelled WAR, but must submit their credentials before receiving volumes from the closely-guarded reserve stock. The subject is indeed becoming of little interest to the average citizen. People at one time took a morbid interest in displays of the uniforms of the armed services, medals, weapons and so forth. Such distasteful exhibits have been replaced by examples depicting the growth of the non-military services. In addition, photographs and scenes revealing the life and work of nonviolent leaders such as Mahatma Gandhi, Martin Luther King and Cesar Chavez draw large crowds.

Teachers and pupils in our schools have become accustomed to a balanced scheme of studies, adapting such innovations as the Peace Education Project to new curricula. A growing input of imaginative literature has largely replaced earlier textbooks which had a strong bias in support of imperialism, exploitation, and the glorification of war. This open and enlightened education has assisted peaceworkers in their persuasion of proprietors of toy and hobby shops to reduce their large stocks of war toys and kits, and to replace them with miniature replicas of constructive machinery and equipment. A Swindon child seen aiming a toy gun at a friend would soon be referred to the Child Guidance Clinic.

Thamesdown is but one example of an area, both at home and abroad, where - through the determined efforts of pacifists and others in the peace movement - militarism in its many aspects has steadily declined. Much remains to be done, but enough has been achieved to ensure success in the future.

Another Point of View

Tony Augarde

The visitor from outer space was allowed time to become acclimatised to the Earth's atmosphere, and was then shown some aspects of our civilisation. On the third day of the tour, the visitor was invited to the Ministry of Defence. The top brass at the Ministry were naturally keen to hear how the visitor's planet equipped its armed forces. The visitor told them: "I think we can pride ourselves that, on our planet, no expense is spared to provide our services with the most up-to-date equipment".

"What sort of guns do you use?" asked one of the generals.

"Guns? Why should we need guns?" The visitor looked puzzled.

"Why, to deal with your enemies".

"Oh yes, our enemies. I suppose they are the same enemies as in all civilised countries: earthquakes, floods, hurricanes, and so on. And of course this is where our army is most useful - a trained group of people ready to rush to any area where there is a disaster, provide medical treatment and food, and help to rebuild shattered homes and communications. But I'm still not sure what you mean about guns. As far as I am aware, the only guns our army uses are to convey lifelines to people stranded in inaccessible places after an earthquake or something like that."

Another general said: "What we really wanted to know was, how are your services armed?"

The visitor replied: "Our services are armed with all the necessary equipment that an army needs - ambulances, field hospitals, mobile kitchens, and all kinds of agricultural machinery to help restore the land after floods and typhoons. Our Cavalry, of course, is specially trained in the use of horses for ploughing; our Engineers are skilled in building roads and bridges; and our Pioneer Corps is expert at digging ditches and sewers; while our Parachute Regiment can be flown to a disaster area anywhere on the planet within a few hours."

"We are very interested to hear about your disaster work", said another general. "Our own forces occasionally do the same thing. But this must be only a small part of your army's work. Can't you tell us more about how they are *usually* employed?"

"Certainly", replied the visitor. "It is true that, thank goodness, there are not so many disasters as to keep our army permanently occupied, and they have plenty of other duties to keep them busy. For example, the Cavalry normally does ploughing and other agricultural jobs at home, and they are often engaged abroad in helping less fortunate countries with *their* agriculture. Similarly, our Catering Corps, besides providing food for hungry people anywhere on our planet, is kept pretty busy at home with its "Meals on wheels" scheme that delivers regular meals to old people and invalids who can't cook for themselves but want to remain fairly independent. The Signals Corps likewise helps old people by fixing up free telephones and radios for them. Yet another example is the Education Corps, which helps illiterates all over the planet to learn to read and write, following methods which - I learnt yesterday - are similar to those of someone on your own planet called Paulo Freire."

By this time, some of the military men were becoming restless. One of them, with ill-concealed impatience, snapped: "This is all very fine, but you still haven't said anything about preparations for conflict".

"I beg your pardon", said the visitor. "You must forgive me for overlooking that very important part of the army's work - preparation for conflict." The generals looked happier.

"We recognise", the visitor continued, "that there is bound to be conflict between people so long as they are different from one another, and that such conflict - while sometimes healthy - can be extremely dangerous. So our Intelligence Corps is given the important task of investigating conflicts and - even more important - foreseeing conflicts. They watch out for areas where injustice or discontent may arise, and try to forestall such dangerous things as inequality of opportunities or the denial of full expression to a minority group. In this way, we can foresee potential conflicts and try to put right any injustice or disagreement before it leads to hostility. Reconciliation is usually possible, as long as a potential conflict is dealt with before bitterness arises."

The generals were impatient again. One of them said curtly, "You still haven't said anything about *war*!"

"What is war?" asked the visitor.

BIBLIOGRAPHY

Suggestions for further reading

1. WHAT IS PACIFISM?

Peter Brock: *Twentieth-Century Pacifism* (Van Nostrand, 1970)
Aldous Huxley: *Ends and Means* (Chatto & Windus, 1937)
Peter Mayer (ed): *The Pacifist Conscience* (Rupert Hart-Davis & Penguin, 1966)
Joan Baez: *Daybreak* (Dial Press, 1968)

2. PACIFISM AND SOCIETY

Arms Trade Helen Collinson: *Death on Delivery* (CAAT, 1989)
Anarchism Ronald Sampson: *Equality and Power* (Heinemann, 1965)
Feminism Dorothy Thompson (ed): *Over Our Dead Bodies* (Virago, 1983)
Lynne Jones: *Keeping the Peace* (The Women's Press, 1983)
Human Rights *Universal Declaration of Human Rights* (UN Dept of Information)
Environment Richard Mabey, Susan Clifford & Angela King (ed): *Second Nature* (Jonathan Cape, 1984)
Christianity H R L 'Dick' Sheppard: *I Will Not Fight* (PPU, 1985)
Clive Barrett: *Peace Together* (James Clarke, 1987)
John Ferguson: *The Politics of Love* (James Clarke, 1974)
Education David Hicks (ed): *Educating for Peace* (Routledge, 1988)
Chris Leeds: *Peace and War* (Thornes, 1987)
The Arts Michael Tippett: *Moving into Aquarius* (Paladin, 1974)
The Media Crispin Aubrey (ed): *Nukespeak: the Media and the Bomb* (Comedia, 1982)

3. PACIFIST ACTION

Nonviolence R B Gregg: *The Power of Nonviolence* (James Clarke, 1960)
Robert Seeley: *Handbook of Nonviolence* (Lawrence Hill, 1986)
Conscientious Objection David Boulton: *Objection Overruled* (MacGibbon & Kee, 1967)
Denis Hayes: *Challenge of Conscience* (Allen & Unwin, 1949)
Peter Chrisp: *Conscientious Objectors* (Tressell, 1989)
Northern Ireland Denis Barritt: *Northern Ireland: a Problem to Every Solution* (Quaker Peace & Service, 1982)

4. ALTERNATIVES

Co-operation Mildred Masheder: *Let's Co-Operate* (PPU, 1986)
Community W H G Armytage: *Heavens Below* (Routledge, 1961)
Lifestyle Erik Dammann: *The Future in our Hands* (Pergamon, 1979)

George Lakey: *Strategy for a Living Revolution* (W H Freeman, 1973)
Vegetarianism Mark Gold: *Living without Cruelty* (Greenprint, 1988)
Katharine Clements: *Why Vegan?* (Heretic Books, 1985)
The Vegetarian (magazine), Vegetarian Society, Parkdale, Dunham Road, Altrincham, Cheshire WA14 4QG
Alternative Technology F Schumacher: *Small is Beautiful* (Abacus, 1974)

5. PEACEMAKERS
Gandhi M K Gandhi: *An Autobiography, or The Story of my Experiments with Truth* (Navajivan, 1927)
Joan Bondurant: *Conquest of Violence* (University of California Press, 1958)
Martin Luther King M L King: *Trumpet of Conscience* (Harper & Row, 1968)
M L King: *Strength to Love* (Harper & Row, 1968)
Patricia Baker: *Martin Luther King* (Wayland, 1974)
Danilo Dolci James McNeish: *Fire under the Ashes* (Hodder, 1965)
Danilo Dolci: *Poverty in Sicily* (Penguin, 1973)
Tolstoy Ronald Sampson: *Tolstoy on the Causes of War* (PPU, 1987)
Leo Tolstoy: *The Inevitable Revolution* (Housmans, 1981)
Leo Tolstoy: *The Kingdom of God and Peace Essays* (OUP, 1960)
Vera Brittain Winifred and Alan Eden-Green (ed): *Testament of a Peace-Lover* (Virago, 1988)
Yvonne Bennett: *Vera Brittain: Women and Peace* (PPU, 1987)

6. PACIFIST ORGANISATIONS
Peace Pledge Union Sybil Morrison: *I Renounce War* (Sheppard Press, 1962)
Bill Hetherington: *Resisting War: 50 Years Working for Peace* (PPU 1986)
Dick Sheppard: *I Will Not Fight* (PPU, 1985)
Carolyn Scott: *Dick Sheppard* (Hodder, 1977)
Sybil Morrison: *The Life and Work of Stuart Morris* (PPU, 1969)

7. THE FUTURE
William Morris: *News from Nowhere* (Routledge, 1970)

Many of these publications can be obtained from the Peace Pledge Union, Dick Sheppard House, 6 Endsleigh Street, London WC1H 0DX (telephone 071-387-5501) or from Housmans Bookshop, 5 Caledonian Road, King's Cross, London N1 9DX (telephone 071-837-4473). Books may be borrowed for a small fee through the Inter-Library Loan Service: enquire at your local library. There is also a comprehensive library at the School of Peace Studies, University of Bradford, Bradford 7, West Yorkshire BD7 1DP (telephone 0274-733466).

Notes on Contributors

Sir Michael Tippett The distinguished composer, who went to prison as a conscientious objector in the Second World War, is President of the Peace Pledge Union.

Tony Augarde A member of the Peace Pledge Union's Campaign and Development Committee, Tony is also Departmental Manager of the English Dictionaries at the Oxford University Press and author of *The Oxford Guide to Word Games*.

Joan Baez American folk-singer noted not only for performing such songs as *We Shall Overcome* but also for her involvement in the peace movement, from opposition to the Vietnam War to resisting war taxes. In 1965 she founded the Institute for the Study of Nonviolence, near her home in California.

William Hetherington A social worker by profession who became a pacifist after National Service in the Navy. He writes regularly for PPU publications, is the PPU's honorary archivist and has represented the PPU in court hearings arising from War Tax Resistance. He has experience of nonviolent actions in Britain, Northern Ireland, and many parts of both East and West Europe.

Hilda Morris Was married to the late Stuart Morris, for many years the Hon Secretary of the PPU. She writes regular articles on the international scene.

Dr Vernon Cutting Formerly Secretary of the World Development Movement, he worked in agricultural research and education in Malawi for 15 years. Overseas interests continued at Long Ashton Research Station, University of Bristol, and on UNESCO assignments in Asia and Africa.

Paul Seed PPU member and lifelong pacifist who has been actively involved with the Campaign against Arms Trade (CAAT) since it was set up.

Tom Woodhouse Has worked at the School of Peace Studies at Bradford University since 1974. He is editor of *Peace Research Reports* and has written about labour and social history, industrial democracy and arms conversion.

Mulford Sibley Professor of Political Science at the University of Minnesota, he co-wrote *Conscription of Conscience* and edited *The Quiet Battle*, an anthology on nonviolence.

Ronald Sampson Used to teach 'politics' students: he wrote *Equality and Power* (1965) and *Tolstoy: the Discovery of Peace* (1973). His family includes bees - and a horse, now like himself very old.

Rachel Hope Author of *Women, Militarism and Nonviolence* (PPU).

Jan Melichar A former refugee from Czechoslovakia who now works at the Peace Pledge Union's headquarters and is involved in developing its 'Children and War' project.

James Gordon Brought up as a Roman Catholic, he later moved to the

Society of Friends. Campaigner for racial equality; Community Relations Officer in Cambridge, 1976-80. Since 1988, Policy Development and Information Officer, Greater London Action for Race Equality.

Ian Davis Convenor of the Green Party's Working Group on Defence.

Kim Taplin A Christian pacifist and writer on conservation and rural subjects; author of *The English Path* and *Tongues in Trees*.

Dr Alan Litherland A Methodist and former Chairman of the Fellowship of Reconciliation; author of *War under Judgement* (Fellowship of Reconciliation, 1978).

Christopher Titmuss Formerly a Buddhist monk in Thailand and India, 1970-76. Co-founder of Gaia House, an international Retreat Centre in Devon.

Howard Clark Was co-editor of *Peace News* from 1971-76, and is the author or co-author of books on nonviolent direct action. Currently a member of staff at the headquarters of the War Resisters' International, in London.

Will Warren Quaker and pacifist who went to Belfast in the early 1970s to spend his retirement as a nonviolent reconciler in Northern Ireland. He moved to Londonderry and stayed there for six years, helping the children and supporting those affected by intimidation. After his death, a house renovated by Derry Youth and Community Workshop was dedicated in his memory.

Diderich H Lund Member of the Norwegian section of War Resisters' International, he was active from 1940 to 1944 in the Norwegian resistance to the Nazis.

Lucy Beck Comes from a Quaker pacifist background and has worked for the Society of Friends and then for the Peace Pledge Union from 1975 to 1986. She helped to develop the PPU's Remembrance Campaign.

James McCarthy Was formerly in charge of the PPU's Peace Education Project. Associated with the Peace Education Network.

Adam Curle Was the first Professor of Peace Studies at Bradford University. Previously he taught philosophy at Oxford and Exeter. Spent 20 years overseas as consultant to governments in Asia and Africa.

James O'Connell Professor of Peace Studies at Bradford University.

Mildred Masheder Author of books on co-operative activities for children and adults.

Cyril Wright Conscientious objector who has recorded his experiences on tape for the Imperial War Museum. Spent ten years as community farmworker and market gardener. Then teacher. Active with the PPU since its inception.

Mike Thomas Organiser for the UK of "Future in our Hands" with headquarters at 120 York Road, Swindon, Wilts.

Swindon Pulse Wholefood Co-Op Has a shop in Swindon for the sale of organic products - fruit, vegetables, wine, domestic items, and for publications. Curtis Street, Swindon, Wilts.

Roger Kelly Director of the Centre for Alternative Technology, Machynlleth, Powys, Wales.

Harry Mister Former distribution manager of *Peace News* and manager of Housmans Bookshop in London. Now secretary of Peace News Trustees.

INDEX